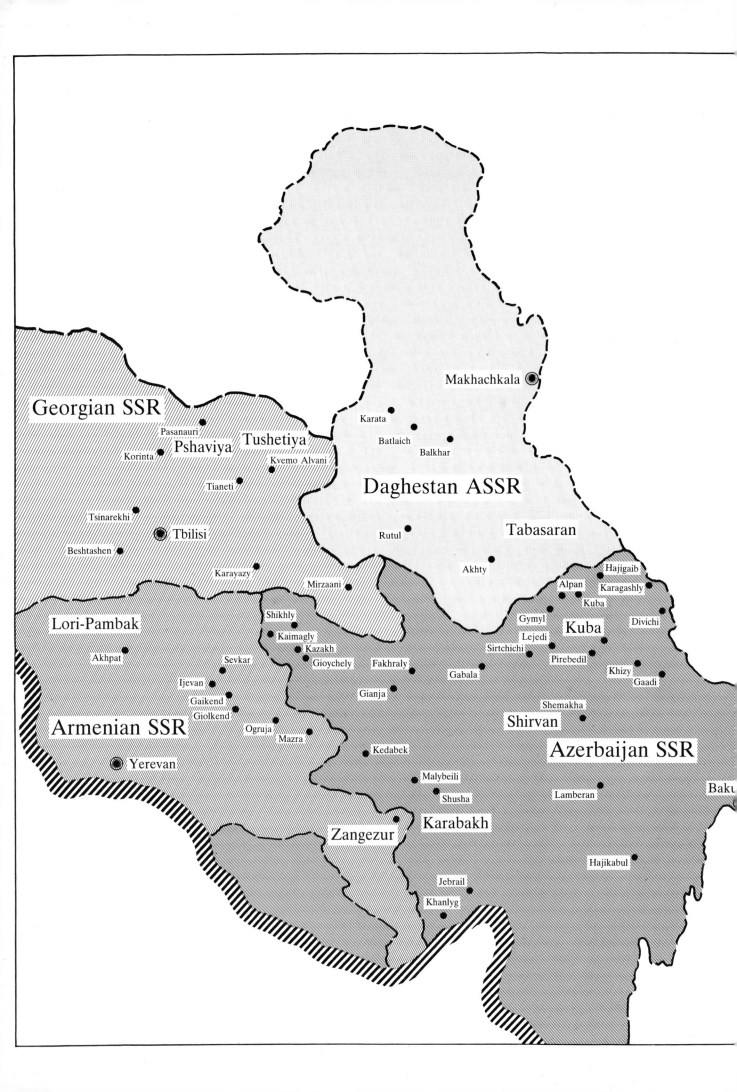

Liatif Kerimov • Nonna Stepanian • Tatyana Grigoliya • David Tsitsishvili

RUGS & CARPETS FROM THE CAUCASUS

The Russian Collections

ALLEN LANE / PENGUIN BOOKS
AURORA ART PUBLISHERS, LENINGRAD

Designed by Irina Luzhina

Translated from the Russian by Arthur
Shkarovsky-Raffé

The Publishers are grateful to Mr. David
Black and Mr. Clive Loveless for their
invaluable advice

Penguin Books Ltd, Harmondsworth,
Middlesex, England

Penguin Books, 40 West 23rd Street, New York,
New York 10010, U.S.A.

Penguin Books Australia Ltd, Ringwood,
Victoria, Australia

Penguin Books Canada Ltd, 2801 John Street, Markham,
Ontario, Canada L3R 1B4

Penguin Books (N.Z.) Ltd, 182–190 Wairau Road,
Auckland 10, New Zealand

Published by Allen Lane/Penguin Books 1984

Copyright © Aurora Art Publishers, Leningrad, 1984

Created by Aurora Art Publishers, Leningrad, for joint
publication of Aurora and Penguin Books Limited /
Allen Lane

Penguin ISBN 014 00 6370 6

Allen Lane ISBN 0 7139 1505 6

Printed and bound in Austria by Globus, Vienna

Carpet weaving, like any other decorative and applied art, graphically illustrates, in its fusion of archaic and modern elements, the temporal and spatial bonds between cultures. It should be noted that in the ornamental composition of rugs and carpets, repeated time and again with few modifications over the centuries, many of the figures and symbols have lost their original meaning and have survived merely as decorative components. Reflected in carpets and rugs, as in pottery, metalwork, folk costume and other forms of popular art, are the contacts between different cultures, their intercommunication in commerce and the daily life of various nations and peoples. Curiously enough, religion dominates the decorative and applied arts far less than the visual arts. Thus, a Moslem might have damaged or destroyed a richly illustrated Armenian gospel but would have kept for himself an Armenian carpet or silver filigree bracelet. Similarly, a Christian would hardly keep a copy of the Koran, but would willingly acquire a Persian jug or an Arabic sabre. Moreover, the design and technique of making such foreign items were taken into account whenever the craftsmen of a different creed made a similar object.

Hence, whenever we speak of the Caucasus with its mixture of ethnic groups and religious creeds, with its kaleidoscope of contrasting customs and traditions, and its chequered history, we are unable to attribute to one or another national background any given item of the decorative and applied arts exclusively by the technical features or the place of its making or even the style of the dedication.

The analysis of one-type specimens, provided they are arranged in proper chronological order, may yield definite conclusions. Therefore the ornamental composition of any carpet, whether it be considered in its entirety or from the angle of its various components, should be examined from the aspect of its origin. It is, furthermore, desirable to find for each type of ornament an analogy in other arts. In the case of the rug and carpet we may use for purposes of comparison the illuminations in old manuscripts, the decoration of carved memorial stellae, silver jewellery, embroidery, or block-printed textiles, whose evolution may be continuously traced from the tenth up to the sixteenth century. Finally, we must calculate the frequency with which each type of carpet design was reproduced in one or another definite locality—which is often difficult to do.

5

The universally accepted name of Caucasian rugs and carpets integrates pieces produced for the most part during the nineteenth and early twentieth centuries in the territories of what are now the three Soviet Republics of Azerbaijan, Armenia and Georgia, situated between the Greater Caucasian Range and the Soviet borders with Iran and Turkey. We also include the carpets and rugs made in the highland Autonomous Republic of Daghestan—which is in the Russian Federation, the largest of the Soviet Union Republics—as in style and technique they are akin to those made

in and around Kuba in Azerbaijan. Most Caucasian carpets and rugs were woven in places populated by adherents of Islam under which women were kept in seclusion in women's quarters. They could find an outlet for their creative abilities and energies only in the making of carpets and rugs, which were extensively used in the home mostly to cover the earthen floors. Upon entering a home the host or guest would remove his footwear and, while inside, would sit directly on the floor, either cross-legged or on his haunches. True, in the mountain regions of Azerbaijan and

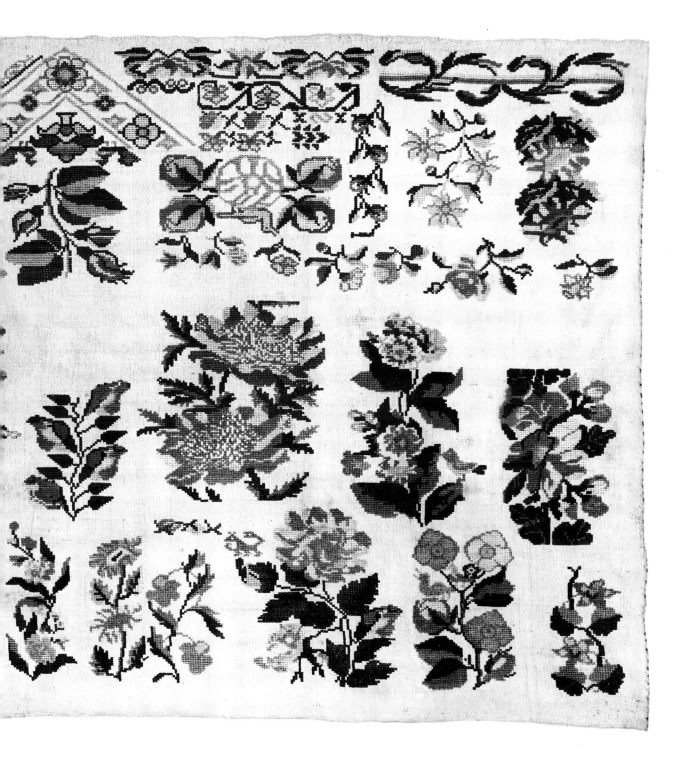

Daghestan, Lezghin and Kiyurin women were not so rigorously confined to the women's quarters; on the other hand, because of the cold a profusion of carpets was needed to keep the house warm.

The Armenians and Georgians who professed the Christian faith were not called upon by religion to restrict women's freedom of movement. Here the climate and the customs played a decisive role in the development of carpet weaving. In the colder highlands of Armenia mostly pile carpets were made; in warmer Georgia flat-woven items were mainly produced.

Interest in Caucasian rugs and carpets has markedly increased over the last ten years or so. Collectors and carpet scholars have been attracted by a diversity of types, bold patterning, and a subtle harmony of colour schemes. Most exciting is the uniqueness of each of the carpets woven just before the turn of the twentieth century, after which the making of many identical items from a printed design came into practice.

Caucasian rugs and carpets reached the European markets more often than not under different names, derived either from the name of the village where they were made or, more seldom, from the type of design. Yet since European carpet vendors usually had no direct contact with the makers, it was often the case, even in special handbooks on carpets, to discover curious paradoxes. *The Handbook of Oriental Carpets* by Neugebauer and Orendi (published in Leipzig in 1923) provides examples of such confusions: plate No. 85 depicts a typical carpet from the village of Chichi near Kuba in Azerbaijan. However, it is defined as a Shirvan and is said to be sold as a Daghestan, a Mecca (?!) or merely as a Persian carpet; plate No. 86 shows a carpet with the Khilabuta design made in the village of Amirajan (Khila) near Baku in Azerbaijan. Again it is defined as a Shirvan and is said to be sold as a Daghestan, a Baku or simply a Persian carpet. In recent publications such major errors in the attribution of carpet design are much fewer. This is largely due to the monograph written by Liatif Kerimov, one of the authors of the present book. His book *The Azerbaijanian Carpet* (published in Russian) listed and defined as many as 1,400 ornamental motifs, border compositions and complete carpet designs. Though this has made possible a more exact establishment of the place of origin of virtually every Azerbaijanian carpet, in some publications inaccurate definitions still occur.

In this book, the authors, without taking on such a formidable task as the analysis of the origin of the various ornamental motifs present in Caucasian carpets and rugs, provide a selection of the more typical of these pieces from the museums of Baku, Makhachkala, Yerevan, Tbilisi, Moscow and Leningrad, and also from some private collections.

To all practical intents there are some carpets and rugs which are no longer encountered—such as the Bakus, Surakhans, Novkhans and Fatmas. In the twentieth century these villages have either been incorporated within the limits of Baku or have

1. Carpet and rug shops in Tiflis in the early 20th century.
From the archives of the Museum of Ethnography of the Peoples of the USSR, Leningrad.

2. Carpet and rug shops in Tiflis in the early 20th century.
From the archives of the Museum of Ethnography of the Peoples of the USSR, Leningrad.

become its suburbs. Likewise no longer encountered is the Karayazy design, as this village has merged with the Georgian town of Gardabani.

Today Azerbaijanian rugs and carpets form the nucleus of all Caucasian weavings. Wherever possible the authors have tried to provide what they understand as the typical specimens of the different regions.

The oldest Caucasian carpets made between the thirteenth and sixteenth centuries are few, for only in the seventeenth and eighteenth centuries did carpet weaving cease to be a court art and become a truly popular art. There are not many pieces datable even to the seventeenth century, because for over two hundred years political circumstances hampered broad development of popular arts, including carpet making. During this period Turkey feuded with Iran for the possession of the Caucasus and at the same time local feudal internecine strife was considerable. Only following the incorporation of the entire Caucasus into the Russian Empire in the early nineteenth century were new roads built and links with European seaports established, making it possible for the rugs and carpets of the Caucasus to reach the international market. Their manufacture then steeply increased, and the nineteenth century became the Golden Age of the Caucasian rug and carpet.

In the first third of the thirteenth century the Mongol-Tartar hordes of Khan Baty overran the Caucasus, wreaking havoc in their path. Some 150 years later the area was once again devastated, this time by the hordes of Tamerlane. From the fifteenth century on Persia warred incessantly with Ottoman Turkey for the possession of the Caucasus. As a result the local population were pauperized, their economy thoroughly disrupted and crafts, including carpet weaving, declined.

Although by the beginning of the seventeenth century the Eastern section of Transcaucasia was nominally part of the Persian Empire, it was by virtue of its remoteness, largely independent. As vassals, these provinces were forced only to pay tribute to Persia and sometimes to send troop contingents. By the second half of the eighteenth century Azerbaijan was a motley pattern of almost twenty larger and smaller khanates enjoying economic and political independence. The most powerful among them were the Shekin, Karabakh, Kuba, Baku, Shirvan and Gianja khanates whose capitals Nukha, Shusha, Kuba, Baku, Shemakha and Gianja subsequently developed into the centres of carpet weaving in the Caucasus.

The khans bent over backwards to imitate the Persian Shah, their feudal overlord. They built palaces in Persian architectural style as, for instance, the still extant palace in Nukha, today Sheki. They had their own court poets, musicians and artists, as well as workshops where girls were instructed in the weaving of carpets after Persian designs, though local artists also composed similar ornaments. The close ties between Persian carpets and those made in the various khanates are observable even today in such names as the Gherati design, or the

Khan design.

In these workshops carpets were woven according to a design done on squared paper by the court artist who was actually the creator of the carpet. The weaver was merely the maker, producing carpets after the same design until the paper on which it was drawn wore out.

A feature specific to the carpet weaver's craft is that, although the maker easily remembers the details of the design of the background and borders, she does this not as one overall pattern but as a definite count sequence. Thus, a weaver knew that to produce the ornamental motif called the *balagyvrym* (small scroll), she had to do one knot in the outline colour, pass seven warp threads and again do an outline knot. Further in this row the design would be knotted automatically. In the next row one knot opening forwards and one knot opening backwards would be done on the knots already there, and so it went row by row. However, the weaver could remember a design count only in its initial position, as the moment it is turned at right angles the count is completely changed. In folk Caucasian carpets ornamental components were woven exclusively in one position. Thus, in the main borders of the carpets reproduced in this book the stylized leaf in both the horizontal and vertical borders is done identically or, in other words, has one and the same count. This is a characteristic feature of the Caucasian carpets.

However, in a mass-produced carpet whose design is drawn on squared paper, with each square a knot, the artist may turn an ornamental motif in any direction desired. A varied, now horizontal, now vertical, position of ornamental components is therefore indicative of a mass-produced piece.

Even after several years of work in the khan's workshop a girl-weaver would know only one or, at best, two designs. Upon marrying she would leave the workshop and continue to weave carpets at home, from now on exclusively from memory. The carpets made for the shah and the khans and for which, as stated earlier, court artists drew the designs, usually had a complex curvilinear pattern difficult to count and to remember. Naturally it was easier for the weaver to memorize designs that consisted only of straight—horizontal, vertical or diagonal—lines. For this reason, when a weaver continued her craft at home she would do solely a geometrized design, simplifying the curvilinear design as best she could. By re-interpreting one or another motif or pattern she herself became creator of the rug or carpet. In short, a geometrized ornamentation is one more characteristic feature common to the folk Caucasian carpets. Also is typical a free placing of the design on the surface of the fabric—which naturally distinguishes it from a carpet woven according to a pre-drawn design. An artist's drawing was usually but a quarter of the overall composition; the completed carpet consisted of four identical parts.

On the other hand, the folk weaver who set the design of background and border by eye alone was not always able to so accurately reproduce it on the frame as the artist did on paper. After a bold start she would not infrequently note that she was

3. Carpet bazaar in Elizavetpol (ancient Gianja, now Kirovabad) in the early 20th century.
From the archives of the Museum of Ethnography of the Peoples of the USSR, Leningrad.

running out of room on the warp and would have to crowd the design, thereby
making the upper portion smaller than the lower one. Purchasers frequently regarded
this lack of symmetry as a shortcoming. Yet it is precisely this free handling of the
design, which is modified in the weaving process, that imparts special appeal to the
folk carpet, as in it one senses the fresh ideas, the creative effort of a real artist rather
than imitative work of a journeyman.

In the Caucasus it was customary for a little girl of seven or eight to help her
mother weave. By the time she married, she would have woven several carpets, as a
rule, a set of three or four, known as the *dast-khali-gebe*, which comprised her dowry.
That special quality of folk craftsmanship, its tradition, derives from the handing
down of designs from mother to daughter and from daughter to granddaughter.
Steeped in the creative atmosphere of domestic carpet weaving, a little girl watched
from her earliest years yarns being spun from amorphous lumps of damp wool, then
being dyed and woven into carpets, saddlebags and *kilims*. In the process she might
find especially beautiful one or another design or colour scheme. If endowed with a
greater talent than that of her mother or sisters, she could improve the design or
pattern taught and, still remaining within the framework of tradition, introduce an
innovation in the family pattern. The gifted weaver would modify the family's
traditional design by adding some small motifs of her own invention, usually

13

geometrically stylized representations of people, animals, birds, such domestic utensils as pitchers, samovars and the like, as well as various inscriptions—in short, precisely those features that make the Caucasian carpet so attractive.

Gifted weavers could not draw a design upon paper until the start of the twentieth century as, until then, it was impossible to procure a sheet of paper in the remote Caucasian hamlets. The pencil, an invention of the nineteenth century, was entirely unknown. Only the village priest or scribe would have paper in his possession and even he would use not pencil but ink; further, only a few could write or draw with a quill or brush. Whenever the weaver sought to preserve an ornamental motif that had taken her fancy, she embroidered it on canvas in cross-stitch, which for her was simpler than drawing. In virtually all Caucasian museums the visitor will see specimens of such designs stitched in coloured silks.

There were cases when the weaver would copy a foreign design, especially when she came across an interesting motif that she could easily repeat by counting from the back. Often she would be asked to make a copy of one or another beautiful carpet. However, none of these folk weavers, even with much experience, could change their own established technique of weaving, knotting, cutting or dyeing. Thus, each village or group of villages in the carpet-making centres had its own design plus a few variations of it or, more seldom, two or three compositionally similar designs.

By virtue of borrowings, nearby villages or groups of villages usually have different but kindred designs. The further apart carpet-making centres are situated from one another, the more pronounced is the difference between their respective designs. As already stated, Caucasian carpets and rugs can be classified according to the basic regions of manufacture, according to their groups, and by types named after the villages where they were manufactured.

The carpets and rugs of different provenance may be distinguished by density, the number of knots per square decimetre and the force with which they were beaten. In some cases the density by weft and by warp is identical, in others the weft density is much greater. There are also differences in the colouring, as not everywhere were the same plants employed to this end. Also of importance is the method of dyeing, as madder with an alum mordant yielded one tinge, while if used with cream of tartar it produced another tint.

Techniques also manifest a pronounced difference, especially in the ratio between the thickness of the yarn used for warp, weft and pile. For this reason some carpets have a rigid fabric while others are soft. In some centres the pile knot is tied by means of a special hooked knife; elsewhere it is tied with fingers alone, which, of course, affects the texture. The yarn also varies in that it might be twisted of two or three strands. In some places exclusively white weft is used, elsewhere it may have been dyed red or blue. The selvedges also vary: in some cases the weft yarn itself forms the selvedges, in others specially dyed yarn is employed. The warp may now and again be spun of a mixture of black and white wool. Fringes have been knotted differently. In some carpets the upper and lower ends have a minute smooth-faced design. Finally, today, in several areas cotton is used in place of wool for warp or weft. All these differences in technical features are so great that the expert can tell the type and origin, and even the name and the design, by touch alone.

The type depends on two salient features, notably design and technique. Yet, how should one classify a piece if an ornamental motif of one region is used in a carpet made elsewhere? If, say, a Kuba-type design is woven in Karabakh or Kazakh, is this a Kazakh, a Karabakh, or a Kuba? It cannot be termed a Karabakh, because it has a Kuba design. Nor can it be termed a Kuba, because it has a different density, pile height and colour scheme. Though in design a real Pirebedil, characteristic of Kuba in Azerbaijan, in colouring and texture it should be termed a Kazakh, although it was woven most likely in the border area of Armenia or Georgia. The authors have tried to provide as typical only specimens which in design, ornamental detail, colour scheme and technique best conform to what it is accepted as an established name. Though it is quite difficult to precisely attribute a carpet they have sought to be as accurate as is humanly possible.

David Tsitsishvili

Rugs and Carpets of Azerbaijan

BY LIATIF KERIMOV

An abundance of raw material and a diversity of local vegetable dyes have from time immemorial contributed to the development of the art of carpet making in Azerbaijan, which lies on the western shores of the Caspian Sea in the eastern part of the Transcaucasus. In this land carpets were used not only to adorn palaces, mosques or the residences of the rich. Every home had its pile-woven *khurjin* saddlebags, *chuval* and *mafrash* storage bags, curtains and hangings. Old-timers claim that in days of yore every Karabakh woman knew how to weave carpets. Indeed, in Azerbaijan today it is difficult to find a home without a carpet, rug, or similar article.

The making of carpets is a time-hallowed example of Azerbaijan's decorative and applied arts, a fact well borne out by both modern archaeological finds made in this Republic and by ancient literary documents. The latter include the writings of the Greek historian Xenophon (fifth century B.C.), the Arab historian El Mukalasi (tenth century B.C.) and the Azerbaijanian poets and classics Ghatran of Tebriz (eleventh century), Nizami of Gianja and Hagani (twelfth century).

By the thirteenth and fourteenth centuries various art objects including carpets that were produced in Azerbaijan attracted the notice of European, specifically Venetian, merchants and travellers, as well as of ambassadors from various countries. It is not surprising, therefore, that from the fifteenth century on we discover Azerbaijanian carpets depicted in the paintings of many European artists, including Carlo Crivelli, Jan van Eyck and Hans Holbein. To this day the beautiful carpets which were woven centuries ago and which are of impeccable technique and quality highlight the collections of the largest of national museums. In fact, most of the world-famous Caucasian carpets—which are of two types: those with a pile comprising the bulk of the carpets that circulate in the world market, and those without one— originate from Azerbaijan.

In Azerbaijanian homes the *khali-gebe*—large, thick, and heavy pile carpets— served as floor coverings for warmth. Flat-woven carpets or *kilims* were used where a more flexible fabric was called for, such as for the *chuval*, *mafrash* and *khurjin* bags which served to store food, bed linen, clothes, household utensils and crockery, for saddle cloths and other purposes. Common among the nomadic tribes were the *khurjin* saddlebags of different sizes, the *chula*, horse and donkey trappings, saddle cloths, sundry coverings or sheaths for smaller articles and little bags in which to keep salt. Today, of course, when Azerbaijanian homes no longer have earthen or stone floors, hand-knotted carpets and other weavings are used more for decoration than for warmth.

The continuity of family tradition, the fact that designs and motifs have been preserved only in the memory of generations of weavers has resulted in the reduction of a countless multitude of designs to approximately 150 basic types. In some non-typical specimens we may, however, find ornamental motifs borrowed from neighbouring districts or even copied from the machine-made carpets of Europe.

There are two ways of making pile carpets. One is to tie the pile thread round the warp threads in the asymmetrical knot; the other—in the symmetrical knot. Flat-woven carpets are made by passing the weft in a simple or complex fashion over the warp threads, or by simply tying the weft round the warp. At least seven different techniques are employed to make flat-woven carpets in Azerbaijan. The list of such carpets includes among others the *palas*, *jejim*, *shadda*, *kilim*, *zili*, *verni* and *sumakh*. Note that these are not place names but the names of the various techniques employed by Azerbaijanian carpet weavers.

Like any work of art the handiwork of the decorative and applied arts and crafts reflect the traditions, customs and the way of life of the people that produces them. The Azerbaijanian carpet is not an exception: its decorative ornaments are a reflection of the environment in which it was created. One finds here representations of people, animals, birds, plants and domestic utensils.

The carpets of Azerbaijan are famed for their beauty, the harmony of their colour scheme, the richness of their pure, bright, radiant and fast dyes. Yet, the colour scheme is restrained and quiet. Dyes were extracted from flowers, roots, leaves and fruit rinds. Thus, yellow tints were obtained from adonis and fig leaves, red and pink from madder and cochineal, pea-green and off-white from onion and apple skins, oak-brown from nutshells, and mid-blue and sky-blue from indigo. To improve the quality of natural dyes alum, salt and several other mordants were used. Folk weavers and dyers had a fine feeling for cold and warm tones and colour contrasts.

As a rule, the central field in most Azerbaijanian carpets is of a dark blue or red; however, one frequently encounters white, cream and sky-blue and, more seldom, green, light brown or black. Whenever the ground of the central field is dark, the ornamental elements are light and bright; whenever it is light the ornamental elements are dark. The same principle applies in the colouring of the various decorative motifs and their outline. In some cases the medallions in the central field are differently coloured than other elements, and mostly contrast with the colouring of the ground. Quite often the ground in the medallions accords with that of the

central field. While the colours of the ground, the central field, and the border vary, the first is necessarily repeated in the ornamentation of the second, thereby producing an overall colour scheme.

In technical and specific artistic features pile and flat-woven carpets may be divided into three basic types—the Kuba-Shirvan, the Gianja-Kazakh and the Karabakh—which are in turn divided into groups and sub-groups.

The Kuba-Shirvans

1. The Kuba group. These include pile carpets common in the neighbourhoods of Kuba (here and later we give for each of the districts mentioned the names of the most popular and common types of carpets), Divichi and Konakhkend.

a) Kuba. Manufactured here are the Kokhna Kuba, Kuba, Alpan, Khyrdangiulchichi, Sirtchichi, Alchagiulchichi, Golluchichi, Gymyl, Gadim Minare and Hajigaib pile carpets, as well as flat-woven *sumakhs*.

b) Divichi. Manufactured here are the Karagashly, Shakhnazarli, Mollakamally, Lejedi, Pirebedil, Herat-Pirebedil, Zeiva, Zagly, Alikhanly, Biliji, Ugakh and Charakh carpets.

c) Konakhkend. Manufactured here are the Orduj, Afurja, Yerfi, Jek, Gyryz, Jimi, Khashy, Konakhkend, Arsalan, Khan and Salmesoyud carpets.

The Kubas profoundly influenced the products of such well-known carpet-making centres of the Kusary region as Khil, Yasab, Imamkulikend and Zeikhur. Although these places are in Azerbaijan proper their carpets are characteristic of Daghestan.

2. The Shirvan group. These include pile carpets common in the neighbourhoods of Shemakha, Maraza, Aksu, Kiurdamir and Hajikabul.

a) Shemakha. Made here are the Shirvan, Kobystan, Shemakha, Israfil and Arjiman carpets.

b) Maraza. Made here are the Maraza, Nabur, Chukhanly, Jagyrly and Jemjemli carpets.

c) Aksu. Made here are the Bijo, Gashed and Pirkhasanly carpets.

d) Kiurdamir. Manufactured here are the Kiurdamir, the Shilyan and the Sor-sor carpets.

e) Hajikabul. Manufactured here are the Hajikabul and Shiralibek pile carpets, and flat-woven *palas* and *kilim*. Also made in this area are the Gabala and Salyan pile carpets, which are similar in design and technique to the Shirvans.

3. The Baku group. These include pile carpets, common in the areas of the Apsheron peninsula and Khizy.

a) Apsheron. Made here are the Baku, Khiliabuta, Khiliaafshan, Surakhany, Novkhany, Geradil, Kala and Fatmai carpets.

b) Khizy. Carpets made here include the pile-woven Fyndygan, the Gaadi, and the flat-woven *zili*.

Despite similar technical features the Kubas, Shirvans and Bakus differ in ornamental designs, the compositions of the Kubas being the most complex.

Representations of people, animals, domestic utensils and other traditional small motifs mainly occur in the Shirvans.

The Kuba Shirvan is usually small, ranging in area from one to four square metres. Occasionally we may find a Kuba-Shirvan from ten to fifteen square metres in area, a twenty square metre carpet being the exception rather than the rule. The density usually ranges from 160,000 to 300,000 knots while there are carpets with as many as 350,000 knots per square metre. Kuba-Shirvans have ornate designs with pleasing heavy flowers and are knotted either in the symmetrical or asymmetrical knot. They have a close but soft pile from three to six millimetres in height.

The Gianja-Kazakhs

1. The Gianja group. These include pile carpets common in the areas of Gianja, Kasum-Ismailov and Kedabek.

a) Gianja. Made here are the Gianja, the Gadim Gianja and the Samukh carpets.

b) Kasum-Ismailov. Made here are the Chaily, Shadly and Fakhraly carpets.

c) Kedabek. The Kedabek and Chirakhly carpets are made here. We may also include in this sub-group the Karagoyunlu carpets, although they are made in the villages of Chaikend and Giolkend in southern Injevan in neighbouring Armenia.

2. The Kazakh group. These include pile carpets common in the neighbourhoods of Kazakh and Borchaly.

a) Kazakh. Made here are the Kazakh, Salakhly, Shikhly, Kemerli, Demirchiler, Kaimagly, Gioychely, Dagkesemen and Oisuzlu pile carpets as well as flat-woven *verni* and *zili*.

b) Borchaly. Carpets made here include the Borchaly, Karayazy, Kachagan and Karachop.

Although the carpet-making centres of the Borchaly region are in Georgia, in designs and technical features their carpets are related to the Gianja-Kazakh carpets.

Though the Gianjas and Kazakhs tend to be similar in technique, they differ in
design, with the ornamentation of the Gianjas being more complex. On the other

hand, the Kazakhs are much larger. The Gianja-Kazakhs range from three to ten square metres in area. Now and again one may encounter in the neighbourhoods of Gianja or Kazakh a set of carpets known as the *dast-khali-gebe* which are characteristic of Karabakh. The Gianja-Kazakhs have simpler compositions than the Kuba-Shirvans, more geometrized designs and restricted colour schemes, frequently employing yellows, greens and brick-reds.

These extremely durable carpets are usually of average dimensions with a density ranging from 60,000 to 120,000 knots per square metre. Both the symmetrical and asymmetrical knots are used. Currently manufactured carpets have a low density but a rather high pile, ranging from six to twelve millimetres.

The Karabakhs

1. The Karabakh group. Included are pile carpets common in the areas of Barda and Agjabedi.

a) Barda. The pile carpets made here include the Barda, Khankarvand, Aran, Goja, Buynuz, Darianur, Achma-Yumma, Shabalytbuta and Balyg. Flat-woven *shadda*, *verni* and *zili* carpets also belong to this group. In technique and design the Nakhichevan carpet also falls within this group.

b) Agjabedi. Made here are the Lamberan, Karabakh and Khantirme pile carpets and flat-woven *jejim*.

2. The Shusha group. This includes such pile carpets as the Malybeili, Lempe, Bagchadagiuller, Bulut, Sakhsydagiuller and Nialbekigiul.

3. The Jebrail group. This includes such pile carpets as the Khanlyg, Karagoyunlu, Gubatly, Kiurd, Gasymushagy, Bakhmenli, Mugan and Talysh and flat-woven *palases* and *kilims*.

The Karabakhs have greatly influenced carpets and other pile and pileless weavings made in the villages of Gadrut, Dashbulag, Tug, Jarabert and Tagla which are located in the Nagorno-Karabakh Autonomous region. The Karabakhs and their three groups of Karabakh proper and Jebrails display similar designs and technical features. Compositions are extremely varied and contain a characteristic geometrized floral design that is more complex than in the Gianja-Kazakhs. The colour scheme is bright and polychromatic, mostly incorporating golden-yellow, crimson, pink, brown and purple. The above mentioned *dast-khali-gebe* carpet set is also common in the Karabakh area.

The Karabakhs are larger than other carpets and are of an elongated shape. As a rule, they range from two to twenty square metres in area but may at times be as

large as twenty-five or thirty square metres. The density is between 90,000 and 160,000 knots per square metre but in some cases there may be a count of 200,000 knots per square metre. Despite a medium or low density of knots the Karabakhs are quite durable and thick. The pile in carpets which are currently manufactured is high ranging from six to ten millimetres.

Carpet weaving in Azerbaijan thrived in the nineteenth century and at the very beginning of the twentieth century after Azerbaijan was incorporated into the Russian Empire. Because of Russia's broad commercial links Azerbaijanian carpets reached world markets and their manufacture increased. These contacts with European markets had adverse effects, though. Firstly, already in the 1880s and 1890s aniline dyes were imported into Transcaucasia and soon became popular because they were simple to use. When, after several years, it was discovered that aniline-dyed woollen yarn faded in the sunshine and when washed, it was too late as the fast vegetable dyes had practically disappeared from use. Secondly, motifs foreign to folk art appeared in the ornamentation of some Caucasian carpets. They were borrowed from factory-produced textiles and embroideries. But strangely enough, it was toilet soap that inflicted the greatest harm in this respect. The Baudelot perfumery company in Moscow, to attract customers, printed on soap wrappings designs for cross-stitched samples and these patterns were borrowed to ornament some carpets as, for example, certain Shushas, such as the Buluts, the Bagchadagiuller and the Sakhsydagiuller.

In Azerbaijan today, as throughout the Orient generally, it is most common to manufacture carpets from designs printed on squared paper. These designs are created by professional artists who draw upon the inexhaustible wealth of folk ornamental art.

In Azerbaijan great effort is made both to encourage weavers' creativity and to preserve the historically vast variety of ornamental design in the folk art of carpet making of all the Caucasian peoples. Thus, the Aliyev Institute of Arts in Baku trains carpet designers, while the Department of Decorative Arts of the Azerbaijanian Institute of Architecture and Art, established nearly thirty-five years ago, elaborates the theoretical aspects of carpet weaving. In 1967 a unique Museum of Carpets and Handicrafts, which exhibits rare carpets of the eighteenth and nineteenth centuries as well as magnificent specimens of virtually all types of Azerbaijanian carpet products, was opened in Baku.

1. KARKHUN PILE CARPET.
218×140 cm

From the village of Karkhun, Yevlah district, Azerbaijan. Early 20th century

Museum of Azerbaijanian Carpets and Handicrafts, Baku. No. 581

Warp: cotton; *weft and pile:* wool.
Knot: symmetrical; *density:* 1,848 knots per dm² (42×44); *pile height:* 5 mm.
Dyes: natural.

Finish: selvedges—wool wrapped round three warps; upper end—2 cm plain weave; lower end—3 cm plain weave.
Ornament and composition: central field displays three medallions with geometrical motifs; framed by three borders.
Not published before.

2. ZILI FLAT-WOVEN CARPET.

200×148 cm

From the village of Khizy, Apsheron district, Azerbaijan. 19th century

Museum of Azerbaijanian Carpets and Handicrafts, Baku. No. 1134

Warp and weft: wool.
Dyes: natural.
Finish: selvedges—wool wrapped round three pairs of warps; upper end—2 cm plain weave; lower end—2.5 cm plain weave ending in fringe.
Ornament and composition: framed central field is checkered with each square containing stylized birds; top and bottom oblongs filled with stylized flowers.
Not published before.

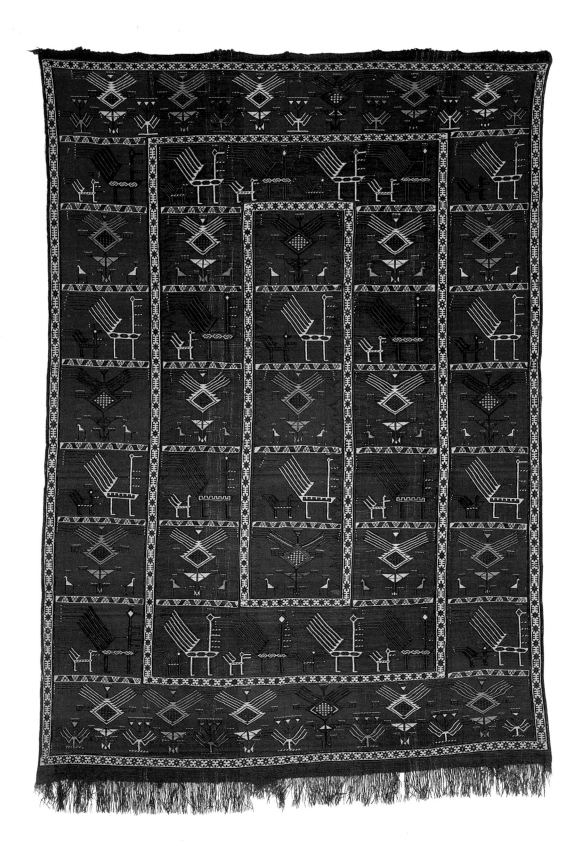

3. ALCHAGIULCHICHI PILE CARPET. 160×114 cm

From the village of Derechichi, Kuba district, Azerbaijan. Early 20th century

Museum of Azerbaijanian Carpets and Handicrafts, Baku. No. 2512

Warp, weft and pile: wool.
Knot: symmetrical; *density:* 2,352 knots per dm² (48×49); *pile height:* 3 mm.
Dyes: natural.

Finish: selvedges—wool wrapped round two pairs of warps; ends—5 mm plain weave ending in fringe.
Ornament and composition: central field contains ten rows of eight-pointed elements and eleven rows composed of figures called the *alchagiul* (cherry plum blossom).
Not published before.

4. ACHMA-YUMMA PILE CARPET.
Detail. 465×140 cm

From the town of Shusha, Azerbaijan. Early 20th century

Museum of Azerbaijanian Carpets and Handicrafts, Baku. No. 595

Warp, weft and pile: wool.
Knot: symmetrical; *density:* 1,520 knots per dm² (40×38); *pile height:* 6 mm.
Dyes: natural and synthetic.
Finish: selvedges—wool wrapped round three warps; ends—2.5 cm plain weave ending in fringe.
Ornament and composition: central field contains seven lozenge-shaped medallions rimmed by open (*achma*) and closed (*yumma*) teeth; also has small geometrical designs; framed by nine borders.
Not published before.

5. KHAN PILE CARPET. 172×129 cm

From the village of Konakhkend, Kuba district, Azerbaijan. 19th century

Museum of the History of Azerbaijan, Baku. No. 3508

Warp, weft and pile: wool.
Knot: symmetrical; *density:* 1,932 knots per dm² (42×46); *pile height:* 4 mm.
Dyes: natural.
Finish: selvedges—wool wrapped round two pairs of warps; ends—1.5 cm plain weave ending in fringe.
Ornament and composition: central field ornamented with a diaper pattern, whose

motifs are arranged symmetrically along the horizontal axis and asymmetrically along the vertical axis.
Not published before.

6. KAIMAGLY PILE CARPET.
290×170 cm

From the village of Kaimagly, Kazakh district, Azerbaijan. 19th century

Museum of Azerbaijanian Carpets and Handicrafts, Baku. No. 659

Warp, weft and pile: wool.

Knot: symmetrical; *density:* 1,330 knots per dm² (35×38); *pile height:* 8 mm.
Dyes: natural.
Finish: selvedges—wool wrapped round three warps; ends—1.5 cm plain weave.
Ornament and composition: central field contains an octagon denoted by a broken line; framed by seven borders with geometrical and stylized floral motifs.
Not published before.

7. SHADDA FLAT-WOVEN CARPET.
103×245 cm

From the village of Lamberan, Barda district, Azerbaijan. 18th century

The Mustafayev Art Museum of Azerbaijan, Baku. No. 793

Warp and weft: wool.
Dyes: natural.
Finish: selvedges—no additional working; ends—wool wrapped round three warps.
Ornament and composition: central field ornamented with a representation of camel caravan; each animal is picked out in different colours; framed by three borders with main one displaying camels, and minor ones, the *zenjire* (chain) motif.
Reproduced is the lower half of the carpet.
Not published before.

8. LEJEDI PILE CARPET. 230×150 cm

From the village of Lejedi, Divichi district, Azerbaijan. Early 20th century

Museum of Azerbaijanian Carpets and Handicrafts, Baku. No. 443

Warp and pile: wool; *weft:* cotton.
Knot: symmetrical; *density:* 2,500 knots per dm² (50×50); *pile height:* 4 mm.
Dyes: natural.

Finish: selvedges—wool wrapped round two pairs of warps; ends—1 cm plain weave.
Ornament and composition: central field contains diaper pattern of stylized floral motifs; framed by five borders.
Not published before.

9. UGAKH PILE CARPET.
186×127 cm

From the village of Ugakh, Divichi district, Azerbaijan. First half of 19th century

Liatif Kerimov's collection, Baku

Warp, weft and pile: wool.
Knot: symmetrical; *density:* 2,400 knots per dm² (40×60); *pile height:* 3 mm.
Dyes: natural.

Finish: selvedges—wool wrapped round two pairs of warps; ends—2 cm plain weave ending in fringe.
Ornament and composition: central field ornamented with intricate design, a version of the Golluchichi pattern; framed by four borders.
Not published before.

10. LEMPE PILE CARPET. The centre-piece of *dast-khali-gebe* set. Detail. 570×195 cm

From the town of Shusha, Azerbaijan. 19th century

The Mustafayev Art Museum of Azerbaijan, Baku. No. 650/3

Warp, weft and pile: wool.
Knot: symmetrical; *density:* 1,600 knots per dm² (40×40); *pile height:* 7 mm.
Dyes: natural.
Finish: selvedges—wool wrapped round three warps; ends—1 cm plain weave.

Ornament and composition: central field has a large octagonal medallion; top and bottom parts have medallions that are typical of the given design; scattered throughout field are stylized parrots and flowers.
Not published before.

11. KHANLYG PILE CARPET.
245×162 cm

From the village of Khanlyg, Kubatly district, Azerbaijan. 19th century

The Mustafayev Art Museum of Azerbaijan, Baku. No. 522

Warp, weft and pile: wool.
Knot: symmetrical; *density:* 1,443 knots per dm² (37×39); *pile height:* 5 mm.
Dyes: natural.
Finish: selvedges—wool wrapped round two pairs of warps; ends—0.5 cm plain weave.
Ornament and composition: central field contains a centralized large medallion, four symmetrically disposed quarters of medallions in corners and stylized flowers; framed by three borders.
Not published before.

12. BILIJI PILE CARPET. 132×97 cm

From the village of Biliji, Divichi district, Azerbaijan. 19th century

Museum of the History of Azerbaijan, Baku. No. 1725

Warp, weft and pile: wool.
Knot: symmetrical; *density:* 2,250 knots per dm² (45×50); *pile height:* 3 mm.
Dyes: natural.
Finish: selvedges—wool wrapped round two pairs of warps; ends—2 cm plain weave ending in fringe.

Ornament and composition: central field displays two large elements characteristic of this type of carpets and called the *kheikal;* it also contains crosslike figures and stylized birds and animals; framed by five borders. *Not published before.*

13. ZAGLY PILE CARPET.
290×123 cm

From the vilage of Zagly, Divichi district, Azerbaijan. Early 20th century

Museum of Azerbaijanian Carpets and Handicrafts, Baku. No. 1149

Warp, weft and pile: wool.
Knot: symmetrical; *density:* 2,068 knots per dm² (44×48); *pile height:* 4 mm.
Dyes: natural.
Finish: selvedges—wool wrapped round two pairs of warps; no original ends.
Ornament and composition: central field contains a polyaxial diaper pattern; white elements facing one another are characteristic of such compositional arrangement; central field framed by four borders.
Not published before.

14. KUBA PILE CARPET. 295×150 cm

From the town of Kuba, Azerbaijan. 19th century

Museum of the History of Azerbaijan, Baku. No. 3992

Warp, weft and pile: wool.
Knot: symmetrical; *density:* 2,000 knots per dm² (40×50); *pile height:* 3 mm.
Dyes: natural.
Finish: selvedges—wool wrapped round two pairs of warps; ends—1.5 cm plain weave ending in fringe.
Ornament and composition: central field contains a large elongated hexagon enclosing five medallions; small geometrical elements and stylized birds fill the spaces between the medallions; central field framed by four borders.
Not published before.

15. SIRTCHICHI PILE CARPET.
190×130 cm

From the village of Sirtchichi, Kuba district, Azerbaijan. Late 19th century

Museum of Azerbaijanian Carpets and Handicrafts, Baku. No. 442

Warp and pile: wool; *weft:* cotton.
Knot: symmetrical; *density:* 2,000 knots per dm² (40×50); *pile height:* 3 mm.
Dyes: natural.
Finish: selvedges—wool wrapped round two pairs of warps; no original ends.
Ornament and composition: central field carries rows of *alchagiul* (cherry plum blossom) elements; framed by seven borders.
Not published before.

16. NAMAZLYK-SAF FAMILY PRAYER RUG. 200×152 cm

From the village of Alpan, Kuba district, Azerbaijan. 19th century

The Dzhanashia Museum of Georgia, Tbilisi. No. 2602

Warp, weft and pile: wool.
Knot: symmetrical; *density:* 1,980 knots per dm² (44×45); *pile height:* 1 mm.
Finish: selvedges—wool wrapped round two pairs of warps; ends—2 cm plain weave ending in fringe.
Ornament and composition: consists of four differently ornamented equal parts (*saf* in Arabic means "row"); designed for a family of four; left-hand upper quarter and right-hand lower quarter ornamented with the *gymyl* design; the other two ornamented with the *alpan* design (both designs named after the localities); central field framed by two borders.
Not published before.

17. KUBA *SHAHER* PILE CARPET
(with *shaher* in Arabic meaning "city" or "town"; this implies a carpet woven in a town). 124×90 cm

From the town of Kuba, Azerbaijan. 19th century

The Mustafayev Art Museum of Azerbaijan, Baku. No. 348

Warp, weft, pile: wool.
Knot: symmetrical; *density:* 1,710 knots per dm² (38×45); *pile height:* 4 mm.

Dyes: natural.
Finish: selvedges—wool wrapped round four warps; ends—3 cm plain weave.
Ornament and composition: central field contains a hexagon called the *penjere* (window) which encloses two large elongated medallions; also in central field are geometrical and stylized floral motifs; upper left- and right-hand corners have the date *1233* (of the Hejira).
Not published before.

8. JEMJEMLI PILE CARPET.
160×144 cm

From the village of Jemjemli, Shemakha District, Azerbaijan. 19th century

Museum of Azerbaijanian Carpets and Handicrafts, Baku. No. 2710

Warp, weft and pile: wool.
Knot: symmetrical; *density:* 2,392 knots per 1m² (46×52); *pile height:* 3 mm.

Dyes: natural.
Finish: selvedges—wool wrapped round two pairs of warps; no original ends.
Ornament and composition: central field contains four medallions with geometrical motifs, as well as stylized animals, birds and flowers; framed by five borders.
Not published before.

19. BIJO PILE CARPET. 166×118 cm

From the village of Bijo, Aksu district, Azerbaijan. 19th century

The Dzhanashia Museum of Georgia, Tbilisi. No. 49

Warp and pile: wool; *weft:* wool, mixed with cotton.

Knot: symmetrical; *density:* 1,936 knots per dm² (44×44); *pile height:* 4 mm.

Dyes: natural.

Colours: nine—mid-blue (ground), sky-blue, light blue, white, black, brown, salad-green, dark red, light red.

Finish: selvedges—wool wrapped round two pairs of warps; ends—1 cm plain weave ending in fringe.

Ornament and composition: central field contains three octagonal medallions; secondary elements characteristic exclusively of the Bijo carpets; central field framed by four borders.

Not published before.

20. MUGAN PILE CARPET.
200×90 cm

From the village of Padar, Ali-Bairamli district, Azerbaijan. 19th century

The Dzhanashia Museum of Georgia, Tbilisi. No. 41

Warp, weft and pile: wool.
Knot: symmetrical; *density:* 1,520 per dm² (38×40); *pile height:* 6 mm.
Dyes: natural.
Finish: selvedges—wool wrapped round two pairs of warps; ends—1.5 cm plain weave ending in fringe.
Ornament and composition: unornamented central field framed by four borders characteristic of this type of carpets.
Not published before.

21. HERAT-PIREBEDIL PILE CARPET. 190×126 cm

From the village of Pirebedil, Divichi district, Azerbaijan. Early 20th century

Museum of the History of Azerbaijan, Baku. No. 3500

Warp and weft: cotton; *pile:* wool.
Knot: symmetrical; *density:* 2,250 knots per dm² (45×50); *pile height:* 4 mm.
Dyes: natural.
Colours: five—mid-blue (ground), sky-blue, pink, green, black.
Finish: selvedges—wool wrapped round two pairs of warps; ends—1.5 cm plain weave ending in fringe.

Ornament and composition: central field carries regularly arranged pattern of modified motifs of the *balyg* (fish) design; framed by three borders.
Not published before.

22. KHILIABUTA PILE CARPET. 181×121 cm

From the village of Amirajan, Baku district, Azerbaijan. 19th century

Museum of the History of Azerbaijan, Baku. No. 3987

Warp, weft and pile: wool.
Knot: symmetrical; *density:* 2,000 knots per dm² (40×50); *pile height:* 4 mm.
Dyes: natural.
Finish: selvedges—wool wrapped round two pairs of warps; ends—2.5 cm plain weave ending in fringe.
Ornament and composition: central field displays rows of almond-shaped *buta*, or *boteh*, elements (hence the name of the carpet), a medallion incorporating stylized birds and flowers, and also quarters of medallions in corners; framed by five borders.
Not published before.

23. HASHAD PILE CARPET.

183×125 cm

From the village of Hashad, Aksu district, Azerbaijan. Early 20th century

Museum of Azerbaijanian Carpets and Handicrafts, Baku. No. 1927

Warp, weft and pile: wool.
Knot: symmetrical; *density:* 2,116 knots per dm² (46×46); *pile height:* 4 mm.
Dyes: natural.

Finish: selvedges—wool wrapped round two pairs of warps; upper end—2 cm plain weave; lower end—2.5 cm plain weave.
Ornament and composition: central field contains three large oblongs formed by meandering *zenjire* chain; each oblong disposed amidst stylized animals, flowers and geometrical elements has small centralized rectangle with toothed edges; central field framed by four borders.
Not published before.

24. HAJIGAIB PILE CARPET.
162×108 cm

From the village of Hajigaib, Kuba district, Azerbaijan. Early 20th century

Museum of Azerbaijanian Carpets and Handicrafts, Baku. No. 2418

Warp, weft and pile: wool.
Knot: asymmetrical; *density:* 1,825 knots per dm² (38×48); *pile height:* 4 mm.
Dyes: natural.

Finish: selvedges—wool wrapped round two pairs of warps; no original ends.
Ornament and composition: central field contains three rows of primary and secondary motifs typical of the given pattern; central field framed by three borders.
Not published before.

25. NOVKHANY PILE CARPET.
180×120 cm

From the village of Novkhana, Apsheron district, Azerbaijan. 19th century

The Dzhanashia Museum of Georgia, Tbilisi. No. 34–42/71

Warp, weft and pile: wool.
Knot: symmetrical; *density:* 1,932 knots per dm^2 (42×46); *pile height:* 4 mm.
Dyes: natural.
Finish: selvedges—wool wrapped round three warps; ends—1.5 cm plain weave ending in fringe.

Ornament and composition: central field embellished with seven hexagonal lozenge-shaped medallions of different sizes enclosing smaller medallions that folk weavers call the *koshek ayaghy* (foot of a baby-camel); in large medallions the *koshek ayaghy* is rimmed by twelve round motifs which weavers regard as symbolizing the twelve months; central field also contains stylized birds and geometrical motifs characteristic of the given type of carpets; central field framed by four borders with hook-shaped and floral motifs.
Not published before.

26. KILIM FLAT-WOVEN CARPET.

341×196 cm

From the village of Gobu, Apsheron district, Azerbaijan. Early 20th century

Museum of Azerbaijanian Carpets and Handicrafts, Baku. No. 3128

Warp and weft: wool.
Dyes: natural.
Finish: selvedges—wool wrapped round three pairs of warps; fringe along top and bottom.
Ornament and composition: central field carries horizontal bands alternately filled with geometrical motifs and rhomboidal and triangular patterns.
Not published before.

27. FAKHRALY PILE CARPET.
167×105 cm

From the village of Fakhraly, Kasum-Ismailov district, Azerbaijan. 20th century

The Mustafayev Art Museum of Azerbaijan, Baku. No. 347
Warp, weft and pile: wool.
Knot: symmetrical; *density:* 1,840 knots per dm² (40×46); *pile height:* 5 mm.
Dyes: natural.
Colours: six—mid-blue (ground), light red, pink, ochre, black, green.
Finish: selvedges—wool wrapped round three warps; upper end—1.5 cm plain weave; lower end—5 cm plain weave ending in fringe.
Ornament and composition: at top central field has a mihrab arch (its form borrowed from Islamic architecture) flanked by the date *1342* (of the Hejira); lower is oblong medallion, whose basic ornamental motif consists of stylized weeping willows; central field framed by six borders; main border embellished with a repetitive sequence of a stylized tortoise.
Not published before.

28. GIOYCHELI PILE CARPET.
191×93 cm

From the village of Gioycheli, Kazakh district, Azerbaijan. 20th century

Museum of the History of Azerbaijan, Baku. No. 5178
Warp, weft and pile: wool.
Knot: symmetrical; *density:* 1,200 knots per dm² (30×40); *pile height:* 7 mm.
Dyes: natural.
Colours: eight—red and blue (ground); yellow, white, mauve, green, sky-blue, pink.
Finish: selvedges—wool wrapped round two pairs of warps, ends—3 cm plain weave ending in fringe.
Ornament and composition: central field contains a large elongated medallion filled with geometrical motifs; framed by three borders.
Not published before.

29. ZILI FLAT-WOVEN CARPET.
295×165 cm

From Borchaly district, Georgia. Late 19th century

Museum of Azerbaijanian Carpets and Handicrafts, Baku. No. 868

Warp and weft: wool.
Dyes: natural.
Finish: selvedges—wefts end in fringe; upper end—2 cm plain weave ending in fringe; lower end—2.5 cm plain weave ending in fringe.

Ornament and composition: unornamented central field, framed by fifteen borders.
Not published before.

30. BAKHMENLI PILE CARPET.
236×131 cm

From the village of Khanlyg, Jebrail district, Azerbaijan. Early 20th century

Museum of Azerbaijanian Carpets and Handicrafts, Baku. No. 839

Warp, weft and pile: wool.

Knot: symmetrical; *density:* 1,440 knots per dm^2 (36×40); *pile height:* 7 mm.
Dyes: natural and synthetic.
Finish: selvedges—wool wrapped round two pairs of warps; ends—3 cm plain weave.
Ornament and composition: central field contains figures of original design reminiscent of representation of a tortoise; framed by three borders.
Not published before.

51. KONAKHKEND PILE CARPET.
235×153 cm

From the village of Konakhkend, Kuba District, Azerbaijan. 1948

Museum of Azerbaijanian Carpets and Handicrafts, Baku. No. 337

Warp, weft and pile: wool.
Knot: asymmetrical; *density:* 2,340 knots per dm² (45×52); *pile height:* 4 mm.
Dyes: natural.

Finish: selvedges—wool wrapped round two pairs of warps; ends—1.5 cm plain weave ending in fringe.
Ornament and composition: central field contains a large centralized cruciform medallion, four corner octagonal medallions and four mace-shaped designs; framed by three borders; in the right-hand corner on main border is the date *1948*.
Not published before.

32. GYMYL PILE CARPET.
198×130 cm

From the village of Gymyl, Kuba district, Azerbaijan. 1902

Museum of Azerbaijanian Carpets and Handicrafts, Baku. No. 884
Warp and weft: cotton; *pile:* wool.
Knot: symmetrical; *density:* 2,600 knots per dm² (50×52); *pile height:* 3 mm.
Dyes: natural.
Finish: selvedges—wool wrapped round two pairs of warps; ends—1.5 cm plain weave ending in fringe.
Ornament and composition: central field has a centralized elongated *honcha* medallion (*honcha* means "a present served on a tray"), one of the basic ornamental motifs of this type of carpets, and four corner designs of identical pattern; halfway along the top of central field is the date of manufacture *1902* and an illegible inscription; central field framed by five borders.
Not published before.

33. KHILIASURAKHANY PILE CARPET. 200×110 cm

From the village of Surakhany, Baku district, Azerbaijan. 19th century.

The Dzhanashia Museum of Georgia, Tbilisi. No. 63
Warp, weft and pile: wool.
Knot: symmetrical; *density:* 1,800 knots per dm² (40×45); *pile height:* 5 mm.
Dyes: natural.
Finish: selvedges—wool wrapped round three warps; ends—1.5 cm plain weave ending in fringe.
Ornament and composition: central field contains four medallions of geometrical shape, quarters of identical medallions in corners, *buta* and small geometrical elements; framed by three borders.
Not published before.

34. SUMAKH FLAT-WOVEN CARPET. 291×216 cm

From the town of Kusary, Azerbaijan. Early 20th century

Museum of Azerbaijanian Carpets and Handicrafts, Baku. No. 2589

Warp and weft: wool.
Dyes: natural.

Finish: selvedges—wool wrapped round three warps; ends—3 cm plain weave ending in fringe.
Ornament and composition: central field contains four medallions, two vertical rows of half-medallions and quarters of medallions in corners; framed by four borders.
Not published before.

35. GIANJA PILE CARPET.
306×104 cm

**From the village of Fakhraly, Kasum-Ismailov
district, Azerbaijan. Early 20th century**

Museum of Azerbaijanian Carpets and
Handicrafts, Baku. No. 584

Warp and pile: wool; *weft:* cotton.
Knot: symmetrical; *density:* 1,600 knots per
dm² (40×40); *pile height:* 6 mm.
Dyes: natural.
Finish: selvedges—wool wrapped round three
warps; ends—1.5 cm plain weave ending in
fringe.
Ornament and composition: central field
carries slanting stripes of stylized flowers;
framed by four borders.
Not published before.

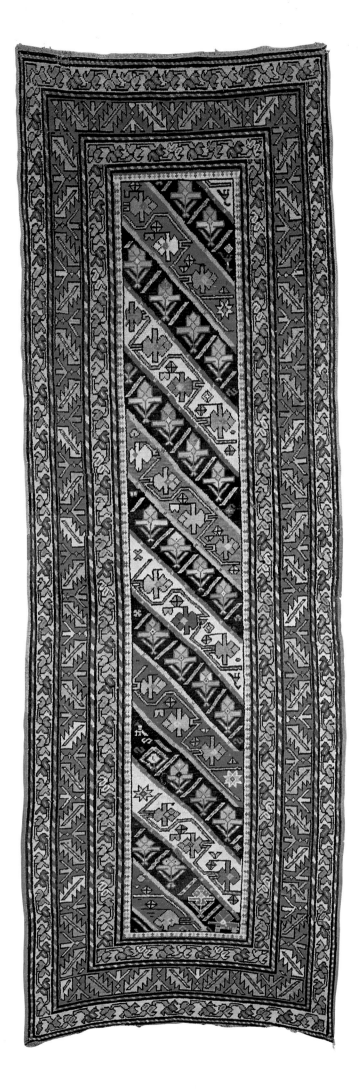

36. JEJIM FLAT-WOVEN CARPET.
188×140 cm

From the town of Jebrail, Azerbaijan. Early 20th century

Museum of Azerbaijanian Carpets and Handicrafts, Baku. No. 4727

Warp and weft: silk.
Dyes: natural and synthetic.

Finish: selvedges—no additional working; ends—cut and sewn with fabric.
Ornament and composition: central field contains alternating narrow vertical bands.
Not published before.

37. KILIM FLAT-WOVEN CARPET.
300×150 cm

From the village of Padar, Ali-Bairamli district, Azerbaijan. 19th century

The Dzhanashia Museum of Georgia, Tbilisi. No. 81

Warp and weft: wool.
Dyes: natural.
Finish: selvedges—no additional working; ends—fringe.
Ornament and composition: framed central field has three longitudinally arranged rows of small medallions characteristic of this type of carpets.
Not published before.

38. FLAT-WOVEN CHII PALAS.
300×204 cm

From the village of Hodjasan, Apsheron district, Azerbaijan. 20th century

Museum of Azerbaijanian Carpets and Handicrafts, Baku. No. 4027

Warp and weft: wool.
Dyes: natural.
Finish: selvedges—wool wrapped round two pairs of warps; fringe along top and bottom.

Ornament and composition: central field contains horizontal bands of varying width with geometrical motifs.
Not published before.

39. FLAT-WOVEN PALAS.
329×144 cm

From the town of Shemakha, Azerbaijan. 20th century

Museum of Azerbaijanian Carpets and Handicrafts, Baku. No. 2553

Warp and weft: wool.
No dyes. Colours of natural wool.
Ornament and composition: pattern of alternating broad and narrow stripes.
Not published before.

40. SUMAKH FLAT-WOVEN CARPET. 340×245 cm

From the town of Kusary, Azerbaijan. Early 20th century

Museum of Azerbaijanian Carpets and Handicrafts, Baku. No. 2627

Warp and weft: wool.
Dyes: natural and synthetic.
Finish: selvedges—wool wrapped round three warps; ends—3 cm plain weave ending in fringe.

Ornament and composition: central field ornamented with three vertical rows of medallions and small geometrical motifs; framed by four borders.
Not published before.

41. HAJIKABUL PILE CARPET.
192×138 cm

From the village of Hajikabul, Ali-Bairamli district, Azerbaijan. 19th century

The Mustafayev Art Museum of Azerbaijan, Baku. No. 599

Warp, weft and pile: wool.
Knot: symmetrical; *density:* 2,150 knots per dm² (43×50); *pile height:* 5 mm.
Finish: selvedges—wool wrapped round two pairs of warps; upper end—2 cm plain weave ending in fringe; lower end—0.5 cm plain weave ending in fringe.

Ornament and composition: central field displays an elongated octagonal medallion characteristic of the given pattern enclosing round motifs called the *alma* (apple); the medallion framed by zigzags comprising a hexagon; elsewhere in the field are geometrical motifs; central field framed by four borders; in the upper right-hand corner broad central border carries the date *1245* (of the Hejira).
Not published before.

42. MARAZA PILE CARPET.
196×146 cm

From the village of Maraza, Shemakha district, Azerbaijan. Early 20th century

Museum of Azerbaijanian Carpets and Handicrafts, Baku. No. 1907

Warp and pile: wool; *weft:* cotton.
Knot: symmetrical; *density:* 2,250 knots per dm² (45×50); *pile height:* 3 mm.
Dyes: natural and synthetic.
Finish: selvedges—wool wrapped round two pairs of warps; ends—1.5 cm plain weave ending in fringe.

Ornament and composition: central field displays broad longitudinal bands ornamented with floral motifs set on a twig known as the *ilangach* (creeping snake); framed by three borders.
Not published before.

43. BUYNUZ PILE CARPET.
210×155 cm

From the town of Shusha, Azerbaijan. 19th century

Museum of Azerbaijanian Carpets and Handicrafts, Baku. No. 318

Warp and pile: wool; *weft:* cotton.
Knot: symmetrical; *density:* 1,260 knots per dm² (36×35); *pile height:* 6 mm.
Dyes: natural.
Finish: selvedges—wool wrapped round three warps; ends—2 cm plain weave ending in fringe.
Ornament and composition: central field ornamented with two vertical rows of the *buynuz* (horn) elements, which give the carpet its name; central field framed by three borders.
Not published before.

44. SHIKHLY PILE CARPET.
314×128 cm

From the village of Shikhly, Kazakh district, Azerbaijan. 19th century

Museum of Azerbaijanian Carpets and Handicrafts, Baku. No. 599

Warp, weft and pile: wool.
Knot: symmetrical; *density:* 1,444 knots per dm² (38×38); *pile height:* 7 mm.
Dyes: natural.
Finish: selvedges—wool wrapped round two pairs of warps; upper end—1.5 cm plain weave; lower end—2 cm plain weave ending in fringe.
Ornament and composition: central field contains three lozenge-shaped medallions enclosing stylized cypresses (considered to be sacred in Azerbaijan) and ducks (symbols of success and prosperity); central field also displays stylized cypresses, animals and small geometrical motifs; framed by five borders.
Not published before.

45. PIREBEDIL PILE CARPET.
171×131 cm

From the village of Pirebedil, Divichi district, Azerbaijan. 19th century

Museum of Arts of Azerbaijan, Baku. No. 334/88

Warp, weft and pile: wool.
Knot: symmetrical; *density:* 2,496 knots per dm² (48×52); *pile height:* 3 mm.
Dyes: natural.
Finish: selvedges—wool wrapped round two pairs of warps; ends—0.5 cm plain weave.
Ornament and composition: central field contains ornamental designs of varied shape and size, with the *buynuz* (horn) motif dominating, and stylized birds; central field framed by six borders.
Not published before.

46. KEZMELI FLAT-WOVEN KILIM.
Detail. 200×350 cm

From the village of Padar, Kazimamedin district, Azerbaijan. 19th century

Liatif Kerimov's collection, Baku
Warp and weft: wool.
Dyes: natural.
Finish: selvedges—no additional working; ends—2 cm plain weave ending in fringe.
Ornament and composition: central field embellished with five large lozenge-shaped medallions set amidst large and small hook-shaped elements; framed by three borders.
Not published before.

47. ALPAN PILE CARPET. 140×86 cm

From the village of Alpan, Kuba district, Azerbaijan. Early 20th century

Museum of Azerbaijanian Carpets and Handicrafts, Baku. No. 1816
Warp and pile: wool; *weft:* cotton.

Knot: symmetrical; *density:* 1,936 knots per dm² (44×44); *pile height:* 4 mm.
Dyes: natural and synthetic.
Finish: selvedges—wool wrapped round three warps; ends—2 cm plain weave.
Ornament and composition: central field contains three polygonal medallions surrounded by slanted *khercheng* (crawfish) motifs; small medallions in corners; central field framed by five borders.
Not published before.

48. KIURDAMIR PILE CARPET.

178×138 cm

From Kiurdamir district, Azerbaijan. 19th century

Museum of Azerbaijanian Carpets and Handicrafts, Baku. No. 565

Warp, weft and pile: wool.
Knot: symmetrical; *density:* 2,115 knots per dm² (45×47); *pile height:* 4 mm.
Dyes: natural.
Finish: selvedges—wool wrapped round three warps; ends—2 cm plain weave ending in fringe.

Ornament and composition: central field shows three lozenge-shaped medallions enclosing crosslike element called *charkh* (wheel) and geometrical motifs; framed by three borders; main border carries a design characteristic of the Shirvan carpets.
Not published before.

49. NAKHICHEVAN PILE CARPET.
250×108 cm

From the town of Ordubad, Azerbaijan. 19th century

Museum of Azerbaijanian Carpets and Handicrafts, Baku. No. 865

Warp, weft and pile: wool.
Knot: symmetrical; *density:* 2,400 knots per dm² (48×50); *pile height:* 4 mm.
Dyes: natural.
Colours: nine—dark blue (ground), light red, sky-blue, green, yellow, ochre, brown, white, black.
Finish: selvedges—wool wrapped round three warps; ends—2 cm plain weave ending in fringe.
Ornament and composition: central field displays geometrical ornament of small lozenges; framed by three borders.
Not published before.

50. SHILYAN PILE CARPET.
164×121 cm

From the village of Shilyan, Kiurdamir district, Azerbaijan. 19th century

Museum of the History of Azerbaijan, Baku. No. 4005

Warp, weft and pile: wool.
Knot: asymmetrical; *density:* 2,250 knots per dm² (45×50); *pile height:* 3 mm.
Dyes: natural.
Finish: selvedges—wool wrapped round two pairs of warps; ends—1.5 cm plain weave ending in fringe.
Ornament and composition: central field ornamented with vertically arranged *shebeke* (lattice) motifs reminiscent of honeycomb and termed the *petek* (beehive); framed by three borders.
Not published before.

51. KARAGASHLY PILE CARPET.
212×133 cm

From Divichi district, Azerbaijan. 20th century

Museum of Azerbaijanian Carpets and Handicrafts, Baku. No. 332

Warp, weft and pile: wool.
Knot: symmetrical; *density:* 1,824 knots per dm² (38×48); *pile height:* 5 mm.
Dyes: natural.
Finish: selvedges—wool wrapped round two pairs of warps; ends—1.5 cm plain weave ending in fringe.
Ornament and composition: central field contains four medallions (characteristic exclusively of the given carpet), stylized animals and birds, a motif called the *chinar* (plane-tree) and round eight-petalled motifs reminiscent of vine leaves (always white); framed by three borders.
Not published before.

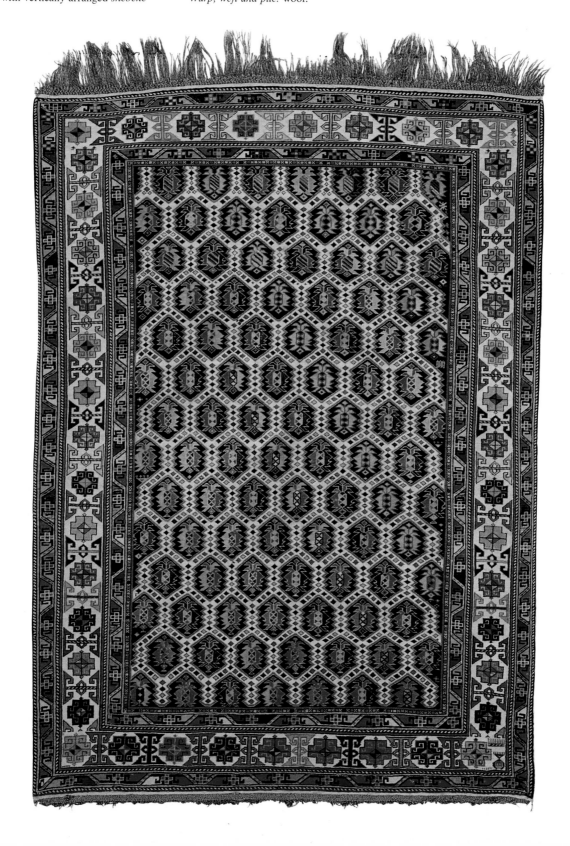

52. SOR-SOR PILE CARPET.
158×118 cm

From the village of Sor-sor, Shemakha district, Azerbaijan. Early 20th century

Museum of Azerbaijanian Carpets and Handicrafts, Baku. No. 378

Warp and pile: wool; *weft:* cotton.
Knot: symmetrical; *density:* 2,035 knots per dm² (35×55); *pile height:* 3 mm.
Dyes: natural.

Finish: selvedges—wool wrapped round two pairs of warps; ends—1.5 cm plain weave ending in fringe.
Ornament and composition: central field contains transverse rows of *buta* elements and mihrab arch; framed by six borders.
Not published before.

3. BIJO PILE CARPET. 153×112 cm

From the village of Bijo, Aksu district, Azerbaijan. Early 20th century

Museum of Azerbaijanian Carpets and Handicrafts, Baku. No. 2199
Warp and pile: wool; *weft:* cotton.
Knot: symmetrical; *density:* 2,068 knots per dm² (44×47); *pile height:* 4 mm.
Dyes: natural.
Finish: selvedges—wool wrapped round two pairs of warps; ends—2 cm plain weave ending in fringe.

Ornament and composition: central field ornamented with diaper patterns of medium size; each diaper contains rectangular motif called the *togga* (belt); flanked by a large crenellated design formed by broken line known as the *kepenek* (butterfly); entire ornamental design framed by band of round motifs termed the *alma* (apple); central field framed by four borders.
Not published before.

54. JEMJEMLI PILE CARPET.
230×90 cm

From the village of Jemjemli, Shemakha district, Azerbaijan. 19th century

The Dzhanashia Museum of Georgia, Tbilisi. No. 47

Warp, weft and pile: wool.
Knot: symmetrical; *density:* 1,892 knots per dm² (44×43); *pile height:* 4 mm.
Dyes: natural.
Finish: selvedges—wool wrapped round two pairs of warps; ends—2 cm plain weave ending in fringe.

Ornament and composition: central field displays four crosslike medallions set amidst geometrical motifs; framed by three borders. *Not published before.*

55. KARABAKH (KHANLYG) PILE CARPET. 341×118 cm

From the town of Shusha, Azerbaijan. 19th century

The Dzhanashia Museum of Georgia, Tbilisi. No. 39

Warp, weft and pile: wool.

Knot: symmetrical; *density:* 1,480 knots per dm² (37×40); *pile height:* 5 mm.
Dyes: natural.
Colours: ten—light red (ground), dark blue (corners, main border and medallions), green, orange, yellow, white, sky-blue, ochre, pink, black.
Finish: selvedges—wool wrapped round three warps; ends—0.5 cm plain weave ending in fringe.
Ornament and composition: central field has large medallion which with top and bottom finials fills most of the field; intricate design composed of floral elements; central field

framed by three borders: main one carries motifs characteristic exclusively of carpets of the given type; minor borders ornamented with the *khamankomanchi* (food greens) that are common to Karabakh carpets.
Not published before.

56. GOLLUCHICHI PILE CARPET.
207×143 cm

From the village of Derechichi, Kuba district, Azerbaijan. 19th century

Museum of Azerbaijanian Carpets and Handicrafts, Baku. No. 481

Warp, weft and pile: wool.
Knot: symmetrical; *density:* 2,494 knots per dm² (43×58); *pile height:* 3 mm.
Dyes: natural.
Finish: selvedges—wool wrapped round two pairs of warps; ends—2 cm plain weave ending in fringe.
Ornament and composition: central field contains four large medallions set on intersection of four large *göl* (sleeve) elements, which give the carpet its name; framed by eleven borders.
Not published before.

57. VERNI FLAT-WOVEN CARPET.
270×220 cm

From Agjabedi district, Azerbaijan. 19th century

Museum of Azerbaijanian Carpets and Handicrafts, Baku. No. 356

Warp and weft: wool.
Dyes: natural.
Finish: selvedges—wool wrapped round three warps; ends—2 cm plain weave.
Ornament and composition: framed central field contains five transverse rows, each having four S-shaped motifs (believed to be dragon symbols).
Not published before.

58. GIANJA PILE CARPET.
280×119 cm

From the town of Gianja, now Kirovabad, Azerbaijan. 19th century

The Dzhanashia Museum of Georgia, Tbilisi. No. 36

Warp, weft and pile: wool.
Knot: symmetrical; *density:* 1,596 knots per dm² (38×42); *pile height:* 5 mm.
Dyes: natural.
Finish: selvedges—wool wrapped round three warps; ends—0.5 cm plain weave ending in fringe.
Ornament and composition: central field incorporates two different elements called the *kohna nakhysh* (old-time design); the element on a white ground is popular in Azerbaijan and characteristic of the ornamentation practised by all Turkic-speaking peoples; twelve indented teeth rimming this element are of symbolical significance—they denote the number of months in the year; central field framed by three borders.
Not published before.

59. GAADI PILE CARPET. 205×95 cm

From the village of Gaadi, Sumgait district, Azerbaijan. 19th century

The Dzhanashia Museum of Georgia, Tbilisi. No. 34–42/74

Warp, weft and pile: wool.
Knot: symmetrical; *density:* 1,980 knots per dm² (44×45); *pile height:* 4 mm.
Dyes: natural.
Finish: selvedges—wool wrapped round three warps; no original ends.
Ornament and composition: central field displays four round medallions; framed by four borders with main one carrying floral motifs composed of broken lines.
Not published before.

60. ARJIMAN PILE CARPET.
340×153 cm

From the village of Arjiman, Baku district, Azerbaijan. 19th century

The Dzhanashia Museum of Georgia, Tbilisi. No. 34–42/73

Warp, weft and pile: wool.
Knot: symmetrical; *density:* 2,300 knots per dm² (46×50); *pile height:* 4 mm.
Dyes: natural.
Finish: selvedges—wool wrapped round two pairs of warps; ends—fringe.
Ornament and composition: central field contains five lozenge-shaped medallions, small geometrical motifs and stylized animals and birds; framed by five borders.
Not published before.

61. KHILIAAFSHAN PILE CARPET.
270×144 cm

From the village of Amirajan, Baku district, Azerbaijan. 19th century

Museum of Azerbaijanian Carpets and Handicrafts, Baku. No. 490

Warp, weft and pile: wool.
Knot: symmetrical; *density:* 1,680 knots per dm² (40×42); *pile height:* 5 mm.
Finish: selvedges—wool wrapped round two pairs of warps; upper end—2.5 cm plain weave ending in fringe; lower end—2 cm plain weave ending in fringe.
Ornament and composition: central field ornamented with symmetrically repeated small medallions, geometrical and floral motifs that are characteristic of the given type of carpet; framed by four borders.
Not published before.

62. GABALA PILE CARPET.
220×127 cm

From the village of Hazry, Kutkashen district, Azerbaijan. Early 20th century

Museum of Azerbaijanian Carpets and Handicrafts, Baku. No. 1431

Warp and pile: wool; *weft:* cotton.
Knot: symmetrical; *density:* 1,672 knots per dm² (38×44); *pile height:* 5 mm.
Dyes: natural and synthetic.
Finish: selvedges—wool wrapped round two pairs of warps; ends—1.5 cm plain weave ending in fringe.
Ornament and composition: central field ornamented with a large medallion with crenellated contour; framed by four borders.
Not published before.

63. SUMAKH FLAT-WOVEN CARPET. 310×249 cm

From the village of Zeikhur, Kusary district, Azerbaijan. 19th century

The Dzhanashia Museum of Georgia, Tbilisi. No. 80

Warp and weft: wool.
Dyes: natural.
Colours: nine—light ochre (ground), dark blue, brown, black, white, yellow, light blue, green, mauve.

Finish: selvedges—no additional working; ends—1 cm plain weave ending in fringe.
Ornament and composition: central field ornamented with the *göl* (sleeve) elements from the *khatai* design (named after the locality) and geometrical motifs; framed by four borders.
Not published before.

**64. NIALBEKIGIUL
(MINAKHANYM) PILE CARPET.**
165×110 cm

**From the town of Shusha, Azerbaijan. Early
20th century**

The Dzhanashia Museum of Georgia, Tbilisi.
No. 34–42/13

Warp, weft and pile: wool.
Knot: symmetrical; *density:* 1,600 knots per
dm² (40×40); *pile height:* 7 mm.
Dyes: natural.

Colours: nine—mid-blue (ground), pink, dark
red, mauve, white, dark blue, yellow, orange,
green.
Finish: selvedges—wool wrapped round three
pairs of warps; ends—1 cm plain weave ending
in fringe.
Ornament and composition: central field
ornamented with floral motifs and round
nialbekigiul (dish-flower motif); framed by
three borders with floral motifs.
Not published before.

65. YAKHARCHIN HORSE TRAPPING. 65×65 cm

From the village of Ugakh, Divichi district, Azerbaijan. 20th century

Liatif Kerimov's collection, Baku

Warp, weft and pile: wool.
Knot: symmetrical; *density:* 2,600 knots per dm² (50×52); *pile height:* 3 mm.
Dyes: natural.
Finish: warps and wefts end in fringe; plaited into tassels.
Ornament and composition: central field contains an octagonal medallion, floral and geometrical motifs; framed by three borders; has two slits for saddle girth.
Not published before.

66. KHURJIN FLAT-WOVEN SADDLEBAGS. 102×35 cm

From the village of Fyndygan, Apsheron district, Azerbaijan. 1940

Museum of Azerbaijanian Carpets and Handicrafts, Baku. No. 406

Warp and weft: wool.
Dyes: natural.
Ornament and composition: the faces of the bags contain centralized roundels; central field framed by three borders; lower bag carries the date *1940.*
Not published before.

67. KHEIBE FLAT-WOVEN SADDLEBAGS. 70×31 cm

From the town of Jebrail, Azerbaijan. Early 20th century

Museum of Azerbaijanian Carpets and Handicrafts, Baku. No. 2689

Warp and weft: wool.
Dyes: natural.
Ornament and composition: central part divided into stripes embellished with geometrical motif; the faces of the bags carry lozenges rimmed with hook-shaped elements.
Not published before.

68. DUZ TORBASY FLAT-WOVEN SALT BAG. 43×31 cm

From the town of Lachin, Azerbaijan. Early 20th century

Museum of Azerbaijanian Carpets and Handicrafts, Baku. No. 3009

Warp and weft: wool.
Dyes: natural.
Colours: five—cream (ground), mid-blue, sky-blue, red, green.
Ornament and composition: framed central field ornamented with diagonal rows of lozenges containing geometrical design.
Not published before.

69. CHANTA FLAT-WOVEN BAG.
25×26 cm

From the town of Shusha, Azerbaijan. 19th century

Museum of Azerbaijanian Carpets and Handicrafts, Baku. No. 1402

Warp and weft: wool.
Dyes: natural.
Colours: five—cream (ground), mid-blue, sky-blue, red, green.
Ornament and composition: central field contains stylized representations of two human figures, birds and geometrical motifs.
Not published before.

70. CHUL FLAT-WOVEN HORSE TRAPPING. 191×180 cm

From the town of Jebrail, Azerbaijan. Early 20th century

The Mustafayev Art Museum of Azerbaijan, Baku. No. 3468

Warp and weft: wool.
Dyes: natural and synthetic.
Finish: selvedges—wool wrapped round two pairs of warps; ends—warps end in fringe; tassels of woollen yarn.
Ornament and composition: lower part is divided into bands of different width with zoomorphic and geometrical elements; upper part embellished with small geometrical and zoomorphic designs; central field framed by one border.
Not published before.

71. DUZ TORBASY FLAT-WOVEN SALT BAG. 70×50 cm

From Kazakh district, Azerbaijan. 19th century

The Dzhanashia Museum of Georgia, Tbilisi. No. 66–26/124

Warp and weft: wool.
Dyes: natural.
Finish: wool wrapped round two pairs of warps.
Ornament and composition: framed central field displays diagonal rows of lozenges, each containing a four-petalled flower; white lozenges comprise a centralized rhomboidal medallion.
Not published before.

Rugs and Carpets
of Daghestan

BY LIATIF KERIMOV

Daghestan, an Autonomous Republic within the Russian Federation, is located on the rocky northern slopes of the Greater Caucasian Range and washed by the Caspian Sea. It is inhabited by about thirty nationalities and ethnographic groups. In this mountainous region sundry arts and crafts such as ornamental stone- and woodcarving, glazed and unglazed ceramics, in addition to carpet weaving, are of ancient origin. To some degree they have been influenced by the arts and crafts of Transcaucasia and the Near East.

As early as the Middle Ages, many Daghestan *auls* (villages) grew into veritable handicraft centres specializing in one particular type of article. The *aul* of Kubachi, for example, is widely known for its jewelled objects and weapons lavishly engraved, damascened and nielloed. Another *aul*, Gotsatl, is famous for its chased copperwork, and yet another, Balkhar, for its unglazed ceramics with slip decoration. The residents of Untsukul have long been engaged in making wooden articles with inlaid patterns of silver and bone. The designs, compositions and colours employed vary from village to village. Worthy of note is the fact that the Kubachi weapons and the Lezghin and Tabasaran carpets were exported to other countries as far back as the tenth—eleventh centuries.

The fact that high-quality wool was available in abundance and that there was also a rich assortment of local vegetable dyes facilitated the extensive development of carpet weaving. Though mostly pile carpets were made, smooth-faced carpets were also woven. In Daghestan as in Azerbaijan pile carpets derive their names from the place of manufacture, as, for instance, the Rutul and the Gasan-Kala. However, there is a difference, as now and again a motif would owe its name to its resemblance to one or another item, as for example, the Topancha, which means "pistol" or the Erpenek, which means "cucumber".

Remarkable for their pliability and expressive ornamentation are flat-woven carpets known locally as *davaghins*. The background is usually dark blue, the central field carries medallions called *rukzals*. The border is nearly always meticulously designed and manifests the same austere hues as the central field.

Among other Daghestanian flat-woven carpets one may mention the *sumakhs*, in which the ends of the weft threads dangle from the back. It should be noted that in colouring and elegance of design these carpets not infrequently excel pile carpets. They have a central field containing three diamond-shaped stepped medallions of equal size. Smaller medallions alternating in a definite sequence flank the ground at regular intervals. Elsewhere the ground is filled with minute motifs, such as rosettes

and eight-pointed stars. The border is composed of one broad band and five to seven narrow secondary stripes. The design of the outer border is always comprised of hooks which are all diagonally disposed in the same direction. The broad band is embellished with an ornament of plant shoots or small medallions containing stylized flowers. The ground is usually brick-red or less often bluish-black.

The best Daghestanian pile carpets, famous for their design and colour scheme, are the Mikrakh, Akhty, Derbent and Tabasaran.

The central field of the Mikrakh and Akhty has three or four medallions, while the border consists of three or five bands. The design of the central medallions is always the same, carrying a large decorative floral motif. Stylized flowers usually fill the spaces in between the medallions of the central field. The angles of the medallions are embellished with arrow-head figures with curvilinear tendrils. The ground is usually dark blue or less often red or ivory.

The Derbents are woven in and around Tabasaran. The central field is embellished with large medallions, either circular or rhomboidal in shape and filled with a geometrical motif. Not infrequently the central field has only one medallion with hooks and eight-pointed stars inscribed within it. A design with a floral motif disposed diagonally on the central field and on the border also occurs. In some cases the central field may be completely covered with intricate dissected medallions in rows of two each. The border, which consists of two to four bands, displays a large geometrical motif and is divided by narrow polychrome stripes. The ground is blue, red or cream.

The traditional forms of decorative and applied art continue to thrive in present-day Daghestan. The craft of carpet making is practised over the length and breadth of the country. Since 1931, a school of carpet making has been turning out specialists in Derbent.

72. DAVAGHIN FLAT-WOVEN CARPET. 410×190 cm

From the village of Karata, Daghestan. 1925

Art Museum, Makhachkala. No. 2812

Warp: cotton; *weft:* wool.
Dyes: synthetic.
Finish: selvedges—no additional working;
ends—warps end in fringe.
Ornament and composition: central field
ornamented with two rows of medallions
edged with hook-shaped elements; framed by
three borders.
Not published before.

73. DAVAGHIN FLAT-WOVEN CARPET. 438×189 cm

From the village of Batlaich, Hunzah district, Daghestan, 1960

Art Museum, Makhachkala. No. 2225

Warp and weft: wool.
Dyes: synthetic.
Finish: selvedges—no additional working; ends—warps end in fringe.
Ornament and composition: central field carries three rows of medallions edged with hook-shaped elements; framed by three borders.
Not published before.

74. FLAT-WOVEN PALAS.
330×165 cm

From the village of Karata, Daghestan. 1962

Art Museum, Makhachkala. No. 2814

Warp and weft: wool.
Dyes: synthetic.
Finish: selvedges—no additional working;
ends—warps end in fringe.
Ornament and composition: central field
ornamented with five rows of small lozenge-
shaped medallions with serrated edges; framed
by three borders.
Not published before.

75. FLAT-WOVEN COT COVERLET.
122×117 cm

**From the village of Khatkhul, Agul district,
Daghestan. 1960s**

Museum of Ethnography of the Peoples of the
USSR, Leningrad. No. 7870–34

Warp and weft: wool.
Dyes: synthetic.
Finish: selvedges—no additional working;
ends—warps end in fringe.
Ornament and composition: central field
carries four times repeated diaper of
geometrical elements; framed by three
borders.
Not published before.

76. FLAT-WOVEN PALAS.
220×135 cm

From the village of Balkhar, Akushin district, Daghestan. 20th century

Museum of the History and Architecture of Daghestan, Makhachkala. No. 17868/Тк. 676

Warp and weft: cotton.
Dyes: natural.
Colours: six—yellow, cherry-red, orange, green, mid-blue, black.

Finish: selvedges—no additional working; ends—fabric sewn on.
Ornament and composition: alternating broad and narrow bands.
Not published before.

77. FLAT-WOVEN BAND FOR CARRYING PITCHERS. 170×6.5 cm

From Daghestan. Mid-20th century

Museum of the History and Architecture of Daghestan, Makhachkala. No. 16365/4/Тк. 496

Warp: cotton; *weft:* wool.
Dyes: synthetic.
Finish: selvedges—no additional working; ends—warps end in fringe.
Ornament and composition: central band, embellished with a repetitive sequence of tripartite geometrical elements, is between two narrow unornamented stripes.
Not published before.

78. KHURJIN FLAT-WOVEN SADDLEBAGS. 110×55 cm

From Daghestan. Late 19th or early 20th century

Museum of the History and Architecture of Daghestan, Makhachkala. No. 1899/Тк. 652

Warp and weft: wool.
Dyes: synthetic.
Colours: twelve—mauve, bright red, orange, pink, violet, mid-blue, light blue, mid-green, dark green, dark brown, mid-brown, white.
Finish: selvedges oversewn; upper end—1.5 cm plain weave, folded and sewn; lower end goes into back.
Ornament and composition: six bands embellished with geometrical pattern; separated by guard stripes of fine broken lines.
Not published before.

79. PILE SADDLE CLOTH. 75×75 cm

From Akhty district, Daghestan. Early 20th century

Museum of the History and Architecture of Daghestan, Makhachkala. No. 26986/Тк. 1034

Warp, weft and pile: wool.
Knot: symmetrical; *density:* 2,925 knots per dm² (45×65); *pile height:* 4 mm.
Dyes: natural.
Finish: selvedges—wool wrapped round six warps; ends—warps end in tasselled fringe.

Ornament and composition: central field displays geometrized floral ornament; framed by three borders with meander design of stylized floral elements.
Not published before.

Carpets of Armenia

BY NONNA STEPANIAN

There is written evidence that carpets were made in Armenia as far back as the eighth century. Thus, in 775–786 the Arab historian ibn-Khaldun described carpets that were manufactured in Armenia and brought to the Baghdad caliphs as annual tribute. According to the tenth-century Arab traveller ibn-Hawqal, the Armenian capital of Dvin, designated as Dabil on Arabic maps, was a centre where magnificent carpets were produced. In his chronicle abu-Avn, another Arab historian, relates that the very word *kali* or *khali*, which all Moslems understand as "carpet", is derived from the name of the Armenian town of Karin or Erzrum, highly respected in the Middle Ages as a centre of arts and crafts. The name of the town of Karin-Kaak, which means the town of Karin, was mispronounced as Kalikala or el Kali (of, or from Karin), and became synonymous with the word *khali*. In his diaries the twelfth-century traveller Marco Polo praised the carpets from these places as the most beautiful in the world.

The few old Armenian carpets extant comprise one of the oldest groups known as dragon carpets, the *vishapagorgs* in Armenian, with *vishap* meaning "dragon" and *gorg*, "carpet". Some eighteenth-century *vishapagorgs* may be seen today in the museums of Berlin, London, Vienna, Budapest, Istanbul and Cairo. There are also some magnificent early specimens in the Museum of the History of Armenia in Yerevan and in the Museum of Ethnography of Armenia in Sardarapat. Characteristic of this group are certain definite motifs, paramount among which is that of a stylized dragon guarding the Tree of Life.

The original character of the *vishapagorg* carpet has long attracted collectors and carpet scholars, but for a long time its origin and dating remained obscure. Despite its affinity to some types of Syrian and Turkish carpets, the link that its ornamental design has with Central Asian art was palpably manifest. Thus, amidst the motifs blended to produce the overall design of archaic *vishapagorgs*, A. Sakisyan, a historian and connoisseur of Oriental carpets, identified motifs of Chinese and Byzantine origin. The winged dragon, stylized lotus blossom and Buddhist symbol could have reached Armenia from China in the late thirteenth and fourteenth centuries during the Mongol-Tartar invasion. To this day Turkish craftsmen call the representation of the lotus flower the *khithayi* which means "from China". On the other hand, the stylized leaf with two tendrils which is reminiscent of the classical acanthus and is known as the *roumi* (Roman?) evidently came from Byzantium.

This intricate amalgam of heterogeneous elements is found exclusively in Armenian art. Study of Armenian carpets of the late eighteenth and early nineteenth centuries, Armenian book illuminations, stone carving and other decorative and applied arts and

crafts contemporary with early specimens of fifteenth–sixteenth century *vishapagorgs*, has enabled scholars to establish their place of manufacture as Armenia. One aid in dating them is their depiction in the works of Florentine and Venetian artists of the fourteenth and fifteenth centuries. Wilhelm van Bode, the first to study the *vishapagorg*, and Alois Riegel after him, maintained that the peculiar colour scheme of these carpets, which were first imported into Italy and subsequently into Holland, influenced the colour scheme of all European painting.

Geometrized to accord with the specific techniques of carpet making, the ornamental motifs of the *vishapagorg* were fused into dynamic medallions. Alternating, the decorative motifs produce mobile yet interlocked systems enclosed within a broad border, wherein the same elements alternate in a quiet sequence. Here is an absolutely correct understanding and realization of the principle of the decorative arts: as in the finest of Persian and Turkoman carpets, the *vishapagorgs* display a splendid balance between motion and repose; the colour scheme, the various hues and contrasts never tire or cloy, because they are akin to Nature's own blends and combinations of colours.

As a rule, archaic *vishapagorgs* have a dark, almost black ground. Light yellows, sky-blues and reds are used to make the pattern stand out clearly against the black background. There is one extant *vishapagorg* with a red ground tinted in the traditional carmine (Vordan Karmir), which historians and chroniclers considered a particularly valuable export item and which the Arab termed "Armenian paint". Adapted to the basic ground colour are all other tints, with the colour scheme each time masterfully executed anew.

A comparison between the compositions of archaic Armenian carpets and later, turn-of-the-twentieth-century carpets of village manufacture well illustrates the extremely tenacious character of the basic motif and colour scheme. The motif of a guardian-dragon protecting the Tree of Life is preserved in popular carpet weaving as a matrix, although it is simplified and reduced to a geometrical outline. An evolution is also manifest in the adaptation of patterns to pieces of diverse format, which is also modified to meet the requirements and needs of everyday life.

The establishment of an autonomous, original carpet pattern in the art of Christianized Armenia is a great achievement. This can be duly appreciated only if one knows the cultural background of the other nations of the Orient which have a well-developed carpet-making industry. These are, firstly, Moslem countries, particularly Iran, where the carpet is seen as a symbol of paradise, and where it has become the basic means for expressing ideas broader than mere aesthetic notions, for example mystical and lyrical formulas of the Koran. These are, secondly, nomadic peoples whose system of ornamental

design evolved in association with the developing tribal *göl* emblem, and for whom carpet weavings fulfilled a most practical function being used to cover floors or serve as various kinds of bags, beds, horse trappings, or even roofings of wagons.

In the way of life of the Armenians who accepted Christianity in 301 as the state religion the carpet did not play so universal a role. Nevertheless, in the fifteenth and sixteenth centuries there existed in Armenia an independent type of carpet, the *vishapagorg*, while the seventeenth century witnessed the appearance of one more composition, the *goar*, named after the weaver who signed her carpet. Subsequently a third type, the *kassakh* appeared in the provinces north of Lake Sevan.

In Armenia embroidery, metalware, jewellery and carpets were produced in towns by artisans united in guilds and by village weavers. Objects of decorative art were also produced in monastery workshops. Armenia's merchant class emerged at an early stage of its history, and merchants were well aware of the market situation when purchasing handicraft objects for export and re-sale. Specific orders were given with the tastes of the customer serving as the guideline, as a result of which traditional carpet design was disrupted. There appeared syncretic composition that combined novel patterns and motifs from carpets of diverse provenance. Repeated time and again, they warrant recording a new syncretic type.

Orientation to changing tastes and the ability to respond to them are as much a property of the decorative crafts and arts as the ability to preserve intact through the years basic imagery and established technique. There is no contradiction here. The borrowing of elements from neighbouring cultures as a feature of the decorative and applied arts of Armenia reflect the history of a nation straddling the crossroads between the Orient and the Occident, of a land that was the scene of continuous strife, frequent partitions and wholesale migration to places often far away.

In the sixteenth century Armenia was divided between Persia and Turkey and its population came to live in that poly-ethnic atmosphere peculiar to the big Oriental empires, which was, naturally, reflected in the arts and crafts, especially in the handicrafts. Yet at the same time the crafts manifested a stability of forms established earlier, a devotion to national imagery and the affiliation of Armenia's culture with the Christian world: representation of the cross, as the basic motif of medieval Armenian art, was introduced into virtually every ornamental design. Finally, there is one more feature characteristic of Armenia's medieval works of art: they frequently have—in a totally different form than was customary in the Near and Middle East—inscriptions in the native tongue. Starting from the seventeenth century with the *goar* carpet noted above,

inscriptions were woven directly into the central field or less often into the border of the carpet. They recorded that the piece was specially devoted to one or another family event, was meant as a gift for a good friend or relation or was woven in memory of someone who had passed away. They also included the year in which the carpet was made, a request to mention the weaver in prayers, and the signature.

The making of carpets during the nineteenth and in the early twentieth centuries developed into a traditional folk craft particularly because it was deeply rooted in the past. Descriptions of the beautiful medieval carpets often occur in Armenian folk tales: for example, the heroine of one of the most well-known, Anait by name, says that she will marry the royal prince only if he masters a useful craft and advises him to learn to weave carpets.

The basic structural principle of the compositional arrangement of most of the Armenian carpets made at the turn of the twentieth century is the division into medallions, which may be of diverse form. They may be rhomboidal, star-shaped, cruciform, fully closed, or be confined to the broken silhouette of a dragon; they might also cover the entire ground in a number of rows, be disposed exclusively along the central axis or "float" in lone isolation on the central field. The central field, borders and medallions contain a multitude of complementary stylized representations: crosses, birds and snakes in combinations with symbols betokening life's eternal circle, such as solar signs, countless types of rosettes, the Tree of Life, plants, domestic animals, horsemen, and people on foot. We may even see the weaver herself holding a comb, as she is also an element of the overall stream of life.

Though one can decode various elements of a carpet's composition, today it is hard to explain the composition in its entirety. The meaning was lost centuries ago, although ethnographers contend that its totemic function as an item used in the home was always borne in mind. Further, evidently the very act of the creation of a carpet had its own symbolic meaning: a girl wove a carpet as part of her dowry and it became a kind of safeguard for her.

In the diaspora Armenians carried with them those types of carpet compositions which historically evolved in their homeland. Thus, in the seventeenth and eighteenth centuries in both Persian and Turkish Armenia one encounters virtually all the traditional types of pile and flat-woven carpets that had been made in the past. Naturally, they bore the imprint of contact with the new surroundings; after all, they were woven in a mixed national environment and any motif traditional for a

neighbouring Azerbaijanian or Kurd village that took the weaver's fancy was easily

introduced. In addition, since carpets comprised a part of the annual tribute collected from the population of Persian or Turkish Armenia, weavers could not ignore Persian and Turkish specimens universally accepted as superior.

After Eastern Armenia was incorporated into the Russian Empire in 1828, carpets began to be purchased from the various centres of manufacture on a systematic basis to be re-sold not only in the larger Caucasian cities of Tiflis, Baku, Alexandropol, Erivan and Shemakha but also in Russia, Europe and America. Special carpet-vending firms were established with branches in St. Petersburg, Moscow, Rostov and Odessa and, at the beginning of the twentieth century, in European and American cities. In short, Caucasian carpets acquired fame and appreciation; they were collected and favoured as part of the furnishings of urban residences.

Meanwhile in Transcaucasian homes in both town and country the carpet-weaving loom was virtually universal, as the making of carpets was an essential supplement to family incomes. At the same time attendant trades developed to deal with the buying and preparation of wool and its dyeing.

Along with the carpets of Azerbaijan and Daghestan those of Armenia comprise a definite group which may be divided into seven sub-groups. The carpets were woven for the most part along the Republic's eastern borders. Thus, in the north we find two kindred sub-groups, the Lori and Pambak; the first includes the Ardvi, Bert, Legan, Agarak, Urut and Chochkan carpets; the second, the Shnokh, Akhpat, Uzunlar, Dzeg and Shagali carpets. Woven between Lake Sevan and the Azerbaijanian border are the carpets of the three sub-groups: the Ijevan, the Shamshadin and the Sevan; the first includes the Ijevan, Agdan, Khashtarak, Sevkar, Uzuntala, Jarkhach and Achajur carpets; the second, the Touzkala, Chinchin and Navur carpets; and the third, the Chaiken, Giolkend, Takhluja and Agbulakh carpets. Still further south we find the Daralagiaz sub-group with centres in the villages of Basargechar, Ogruja, Mazra, Yarpuzlu and Keiti, and the Zangezur sub-group with centres in the town of Goris (Gheriusy) and the villages of Khndzoresk and Dig. This classification was evolved in the first quarter of the twentieth century by M. Ter-Mikayelian, a major authority on carpet weaving in the Caucasus.

In the nineteenth century a large number of pile and flat-woven carpets and other items were made by Kurds living in villages near Erivan and in nomadic encampments in the neighbourhood of Mt. Aragats (Alagioz).

Though Armenian peasant women wove mostly pile carpets, the making of flat-woven items was also common. In most cases these were *kilims* which in Armenia

were called *karpets* but which the Kurds called the *yamani*. *Shadda* and *zili* flat-woven carpets were produced in some Armenian villages in Nagorny Karabakh. Carpets of different types were also woven in Armenian villages located in the neighbouring Georgia and Azerbaijan.

Of special interest are Kurd *yamani* which, due to their fine quality, colouring and relative cheapness, were in great demand throughout the Caucasus. The Kurds also produced an interesting item known as the *chikh*, a type of screen which served as a partition in the tent of the nomadic Kurd. Reed rods which constituted the foundation of the *chikh* were wrapped with multi-coloured woollen threads. Now, however, the Kurds have settled and ceased making carpets for the market.

Currently Armenian hand-knotted carpets are produced in the workshops of the Aigorg firm and as a cottage industry in the villages, where weavers are provided with high-quality yarn dyed in lasting colours and with printed designs evolved by contemporary professionals on the basis of the ancient classical carpets. These carpets find an eager market both at home and abroad.

80. VISHAPAGORG. 230×130 cm

From the town of Alexandropol, today Leninakan, Armenia. 1904

Museum of the Folk Arts of Armenia, Yerevan. No. 3645
Warp, weft and pile: wool.
Knot: asymmetrical; *density:* 900 knots per dm² (30×30); *pile height:* 4 mm.
Dyes: natural and synthetic.
Finish: selvedges—wool wrapped round two pairs of warps; no original ends.

Ornament and composition: central field contains three large polygons enclosed in schematic representations of the *vishap* ("dragon") with *vishaps* between them; also within central field are stylized representations of male figures, animals, birds and small geometrical motifs; a white cartouche on the outer of three borders framing central field has an inscription in Armenian which reads: *1904 . . . Mukaeliants.*
Not published before.

81. VISHAPAGORG. 167×111 cm

**From the town of Alexandropol, today
Leninakan, Armenia. Late 19th century**

Museum of the History of Armenia, Yerevan.
No. 9652

Warp, weft and pile: wool.
Knot: symmetrical; *density:* 750 knots per dm²
(25×30); *pile height:* 6 mm.
Dyes: natural.
Finish: selvedges—wool wrapped round two
pairs of warps; no original ends.

Ornament and composition: central field
contains two octagonal medallions enclosed
within stylized representations of the *vishap*
with another stylized *vishap* between them;
crosses disposed within field; framed by four
borders.
Not published before.

82. MAIN CARPET. 150×115 cm

From the village of Parni, Spitaki district, Armenia. 1869

Museum of the History of Armenia, Yerevan. No. 32

Warp, weft and pile: wool.
Knot: symmetrical; *density:* 625 knots per dm² (25×25); *pile height:* 6 mm.
Dyes: natural.
Finish: selvedges—wool wrapped round two pairs of warps; ends—plain-woven border bands; warps end in twisted double fringe threads.

Ornament and composition: central field contains almond-shaped *buta* figures enclosing crosses; on top an inscription in Armenian reads: *From Akop Mkrtych in the year of 1869*; central field framed by two borders. *Not published before.*

83. MAIN CARPET. 215×127 cm

**From the village of Akhpat, Tumanian
district, Armenia. 19th century**

Museum of the Folk Arts of Armenia,
Yerevan. No. 640

Warp, weft and pile: wool.
Knot: symmetrical; *density:* 750 knots per dm²
(25×30); *pile height:* 5–6 mm.
Dyes: natural.
Colours: five—white, yellow, red, mid-blue,
sky-blue.

Finish: selvedges—wool wrapped round two
pairs of warps; no original ends.
Ornament and composition: central field
contains three rows of variously coloured
serrated polygons with small lozenges carrying
floral design; framed by a broad border.
Not published before.

84. MAIN CARPET. 200×115 cm

From Viots-Dzor, today Yekhegnadzor district, Armenia. 1902

Museum of the Folk Arts of Armenia, Yerevan. No. 2285

Warp, weft and pile: wool.
Knot: symmetrical; *density:* 750 knots per dm² (25×30); *pile height:* 5–6 mm.
Dyes: natural and synthetic.
Colours: four—reddish-brown, yellow, dark brown, white.
Finish: selvedges—wool wrapped round two pairs of warps; no original ends.

Ornament and composition: central field carries three rows of almond-shaped *buta* figures containing Armenian letters; central field framed by four borders; broad band carries the date *1902* above representation of a female figure.
Not published before.

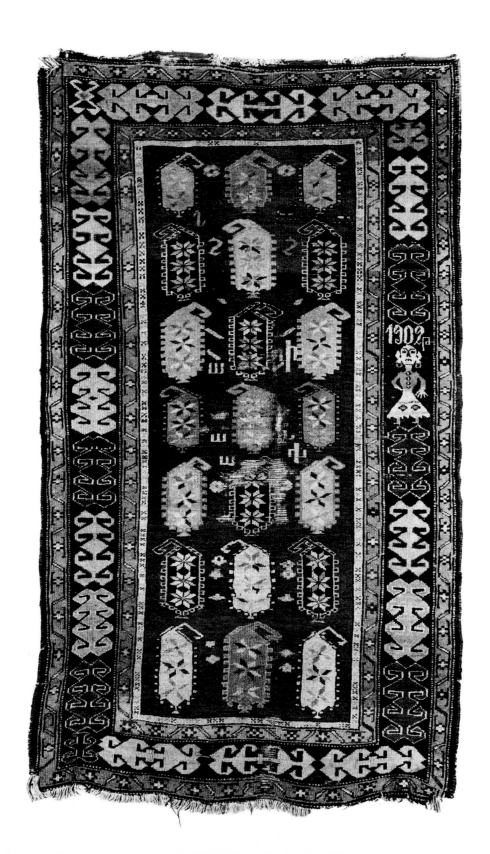

85. MAIN CARPET. 291×106 cm

From Lori-Pambak, today Tumanian district, Armenia. Late 19th century

Museum of the History of Armenia, Yerevan. No. 9368/28

Warp, weft and pile: wool.
Knot: symmetrical; *density:* 500 knots per dm² (20×25); *pile height:* 5–6 mm.
Dyes: natural and synthetic.
Colours: six—black, red, yellow, white, pink, mid-blue.
Finish: selvedges—wool wrapped round four pairs of warps; no original ends.

Ornament and composition: disposed on a black ground are stylized flowers; central field framed by three borders.
Not published before.

86. MAIN CARPET. 350×92 cm

From Sisian district, Armenia. 19th century

Museum of the History of Armenia, Yerevan. No. 9131

Warp, weft and pile: wool.
Knot: symmetrical; *density:* 900 knots per dm² (30×30); *pile height:* 6 mm.

Dyes: natural.
Colours: six—greenish-blue, white, black, sky-blue, red, yellow.
Finish: selvedges—wool wrapped round three pairs of warps; no original ends.
Ornament and composition: central field contains a row of lozenge-shaped medallions, geometrical motifs and stylized birds; framed by three borders carrying geometrical and floral designs.
Not published before.

87. MAIN CARPET. 215×108 cm

From the village of Gadrut, Nagorny Karabakh, Azerbaijan. 1886

Museum of the History of Armenia, Yerevan. No. 9099

Warp, weft and pile: wool.
Knot: symmetrical; *density:* 1,050 knots per dm² (30×35); *pile height:* 4–5 mm.
Dyes: natural and synthetic.
Finish: selvedges—wool wrapped round two pairs of warps; no original ends.
Ornament and composition: central field carries medallions fringed with a serrated strip, cruciform design and representations of animals; on top is the year *1886* and a faded illegible inscription in Armenian; central field framed by three borders.
Not published before.

88. VISHAPAGORG. 224×154 cm

From the village of Khndzoresk, Goris district, Armenia. 19th century

Museum of the History of Armenia, Yerevan. No. 9686

Warp, weft and pile: wool.
Knot: symmetrical; *density:* 1,050 knots per dm² (30×35); *pile height:* 5 mm.
Dyes: natural.
Finish: selvedges—wool wrapped round two pairs of warps; ends—plain weave; warps end in fringe.
Ornament and composition: central field carries three large serrated medallions enclosing stylized crosses; framed by four borders.
Not published before.

89. MAIN CARPET. 240×180 cm

From the village of Verin, Talin district, Armenia. 1897

Museum of the History of Armenia, Yerevan. No. 9543

Warp, weft and pile: wool.
Knot: symmetrical; *density:* 625 knots per dm²
(25×25); *pile height:* 5 mm.
Dyes: natural.
Finish: selvedges—wool wrapped round four pairs of warps; ends—plain weave; fringe of twisted double thread.

Ornament and composition: central field contains three large rhomboidal medallions, inside which—as well as elsewhere in the field—are stylized birds (eagles), floral and geometrical motifs; in the upper part of central field is inscription in Armenian that reads: *1897 Old Rhipsime Marta*; central field framed by six borders.
Not published before.

). MAIN CARPET. 245×131 cm

rom Nagorny Karabakh, Azerbaijan. 1815

Iuseum of the Folk Arts of Armenia,
Ierevan. No. 1600

*I*arp, weft and pile: wool.
*I*not: symmetrical; density: 750 knots per dm²
I5×30); pile height: 5 mm.
*I*yes: natural and synthetic.
*I*inish: selvedges—wool wrapped round two
Iairs of warps; ends—4 cm plain weave.
*I*rnament and composition: central field
Intains row of crosses flanked by rows of

star-shaped medallions enclosing stylized
tarantula-guardian spirits; on top inscription in
Armenian reads: *1815. 10th March Aram
Nakhapetiants*; central field framed by one
border.
Not published before.

91. FLAT-WOVEN KARPET.
250×207 cm

From the village of Dilizhan, Varazhnunik district, Armenia. 19th century

Museum of the History of Armenia, Yerevan. No. 9225

Warp and weft: wool.
Dyes: natural.
Finish: selvedges and ends—wool wrapped round two warps.
Ornament and composition: central field carries longitudinal rows of serrated triangles with floral motifs; framed by a border with floral and crosslike designs.
Published: Davtian, S., *The Armenian Karpet*, Yerevan, 1975, p. 55 (in Armenian).

92. MAIN CARPET. 228×127 cm

From Yekhegnadzor district, Armenia. Late 19th century

Museum of the History of Armenia, Yerevan. No. 7738

Warp, weft and pile: wool.

Knot: symmetrical; *density:* 1,050 knots per dm² (30×35); *pile height:* 4 mm.
Dyes: natural.
Finish: selvedges—wool wrapped round two pairs of warps; ends—plain weave.
Ornament and composition: central field contains three medallions in the shape of stylized crabs, with stylized beetles and branches within each; central field displays representations of human figures, animals, birds and geometrical motifs; framed by three borders.
Not published before.

93. MAIN CARPET. 270×115 cm

From the town of Shusha, Nagorny Karabakh, Azerbaijan. 1886

Museum of the History of Armenia, Yerevan. No. 9052

Warp, weft and pile: wool.
Knot: symmetrical; *density:* 1,400 knots per dm² (40×35); *pile height:* 5 mm.
Dyes: natural and synthetic.
Finish: selvedges—wool wrapped round two warps; ends—plain weave ending in twisted fringe threads.
Ornament and composition: mid-blue central field contains five tarantula-shaped medallions enclosing hexagons and representations of plants, as well as representations of the Tree of Life, flower buds, serpentine and crosslike motifs; central field framed by four borders with geometrical design.
Not published before.

94. VISHAPAGORG. 234×131 cm

From the village of Lambalu, today Shavarshavan, Noyemberian district, Armenia. 19th century

Museum of the History of Armenia, Yerevan. No. 7530

Warp, weft and pile: wool.
Knot: asymmetrical; *density:* 750 knots per dm² (25×30); *pile height:* 5 mm.
Dyes: natural and synthetic.
Finish: selvedges—wool wrapped round three pairs of warps; ends—plain weave; 20 cm long fringe below.
Ornament and composition: central field contains a large centralized rhomboidal medallion enclosed in cruciform frame; stylized *vishap* in each corner; central field framed by three borders.
Not published before.

95. VISHAPAGORG. 286×138 cm

From the village of Jrabert, Nagorny Karabakh, Azerbaijan. Late 19th century

Museum of the History of Armenia, Yerevan. No. 9122

Warp, weft and pile: wool.
Knot: symmetrical; *density:* 500 knots per dm² (20×25); *pile height:* 5 mm.
Dyes: natural and synthetic.
Colours: seven—red, sky-blue, mid-blue, pink, yellow, white, brown.
Finish: selvedges—wool wrapped round four pairs of warps; ends—plain-woven border.
Ornament and composition: red central field contains three octagons enclosing stylized serpentine dragons; each octagon has a square with swastika; central field framed by three borders.
Not published before.

96. VISHAPAGORG. 240×150 cm

From the village of Gadrut, Nagorny Karabakh, Azerbaijan. 18th century

Museum of the History of Armenia, Yerevan. No. 9250

Warp, weft and pile: wool.
Knot: symmetrical; *density:* 1,400 knots per dm² (40×35); *pile height:* 5 mm.
Dyes: natural.
Finish: selvedges—wool wrapped round two pairs of warps; ends—plain weave.
Ornament and composition: light-red central field contains two and a half polygons enclosing stylized dragons with centralized squares with the swastika motif; also within central field are stylized representations of human figures, animals and birds; central field framed by three borders.
Not published before.

97. MAIN CARPET. 305×112 cm

From Erivan, today Yerevan, Armenia. 19th century

Museum of the History of Armenia, Yerevan. No. 8057/32

Warp, weft and pile: wool.
Knot: symmetrical; *density:* 840 knots per dm² (28×30); *pile height:* 6 mm.
Dyes: natural and synthetic.
Finish: selvedges—wool wrapped round warps; no original ends.
Ornament and composition: central field carries five rows of large *buta* figures

containing flowers and small crosses; framed by three borders; main border ornamented with floral motif; minor ones carry floral-meander pattern.
Not published before.

98. LORI CARPET. 292×122 cm

From the village of Lori, Tumanian district, Armenia. 1791

Museum of the History of Armenia, Yerevan. No. 7739

Warp, weft and pile: wool.

Knot: symmetrical; *density:* 500 knots per dm² (20×25); *pile height:* 6 mm.
Dyes: natural.
Finish: selvedges—wool wrapped round three pairs of warps; ends—plain-woven border; fringe of twisted double thread.
Ornament and composition: central field contains rows of vessels holding red flowers and sprays of blossoming lilac; between vessels representations of plants and animals; upper portion of this carpet (cental part of which has been restored) has the year *1791*; central field framed by a broad border with floral design.
Not published before.

99. MAIN CARPET. 350×105 cm

From the village of Chartar, Nagorny Karabakh, Azerbaijan. Late 19th century

Museum of the History of Armenia, Yerevan. No. 10225

Warp, weft and pile: wool.
Knot: symmetrical; *density:* 750 knots per dm² (25×30); *pile height:* 5 mm.
Dyes: natural.
Finish: selvedges—wool wrapped round two warps; ends—plain weave.
Ornament and composition: central field contains a row of hexagonal medallions enclosing lozenges, stylized birds and crosses; framed by three borders.
Not published before.

100. MAIN CARPET. 242×133 cm

From the village of Gadrut, Nagorny Karabakh, Azerbaijan. 19th century

Museum of the History of Armenia, Yerevan. No. 9134

Warp, weft and pile: wool.
Knot: symmetrical; *density:* 840 knots per dm² (28×30); *pile height:* 5 mm.
Dyes: natural.
Finish: selvedges—wool wrapped round two warps; ends—plain weave.
Ornament and composition: central field contains three rows of almond-shaped *buta* designs enclosed in small stylized crosses; inscribed within the *buta* designs and also between them are stylized representations of the Tree of Life; central field framed by three borders.
Not published before.

101. MAIN CARPET. 235×125 cm

From the village of Chinar, Shamshadin district, Armenia. 1946

Museum of the History of Armenia, Yerevan. No. 10245

Warp, weft and pile: wool.
Knot: symmetrical; *density:* 750 knots per dm² (25×30); *pile height:* 3 mm.
Dyes: natural and synthetic.
Colours: six—red, khaki, mid-blue, brown, mauve, light green.
Finish: selvedges—wool wrapped round three pairs of warps; ends—strengthened by fabric.
Ornament and composition: central field contains three hexagons with stylized crosses centrally positioned within each; crosses carry stylized representations of the Tree of Life; elsewhere in the central field are stylized animals, birds and small crosses; central field framed by two borders.
Not published before.

102. MAIN CARPET. 230×154 cm

From the village of Sevkar, Ijevan district, Armenia. Early 19th century

Museum of the History of Armenia, Yerevan. No. 7622/30

Warp, weft and pile: wool.
Knot: symmetrical; *density:* 550 knots per dm² (22×25); *pile height:* 5–6 mm.
Dyes: natural.
Colours: three—dark pink, green, mid-blue.
Finish: selvedges—wool wrapped round two pairs of warps; no original ends.
Ornament and composition: central field contains two cruciform medallions enclosing zigzag-framed lozenges, floral motifs and representations of birds; framed by a broad border ornamented with crosses.
Not published before.

103. MAIN CARPET. 170×116 cm

From the town of Shusha, Nagorny Karabakh, Azerbaijan. 1910

Museum of the History of Armenia, Yerevan. No. 9247

Warp, weft and pile: wool.
Knot: symmetrical; *density:* 810 knots per dm² (27×30); *pile height:* 5 mm.
Dyes: natural.
Finish: selvedges and lower end—wool wrapped round two pairs of warps; no original upper end.
Ornament and composition: central field contains two rows of representations of the Tree of Life flanking central row of lozenge-type figures fringed with hooks and geometrical motifs; elsewhere in central field, framed by three borders, are eight-pointed stars, small crosses, zoomorphic designs and stylized swastikas.
Not published before.

104. MAIN CARPET. 320×105 cm

From the village of Oshakan, Ashtarak district, Armenia. 19th century

Museum of the History of Armenia, Yerevan. No. 9245

Warp, weft and pile: wool.
Knot: symmetrical; *density:* 750 knots per dm² (25×30); *pile height:* 5–6 mm.
Dyes: natural.
Finish: selvedges—wool wrapped round two pairs of warps; no original ends.
Ornament and composition: central field carries three elongated hexagons enclosing smaller ones with stylized crosses; framed by three borders.
Not published before.

105. FLAT-WOVEN KHURJIN SADDLEBAGS. 125×46 cm

From the town of Alexandropol, today Leninakan, Armenia. 19th century

Museum of the History of Armenia, Yerevan. No. 8107

Warp and weft: wool.
Dyes: natural.
Ornament and composition: large hexagons with hooks on a white ground; on either side of hexagons three bands with geometrical design; two hexagons with hooks on a red ground.
Not published before.

106. FLAT-WOVEN HORSE CLOTH

(*zili* technique). 138×110 cm

From the village of Lori, Tumanian district, Armenia. 1887

Museum of the History of Armenia, Yerevan. No. 1996

Warp and weft: wool.
Dyes: natural.
Finish: wool wrapped round two edge warps; tassels below.
Ornament and composition: horizontal bands carrying stylized representations of people, animals, birds, crosses and carpetweaver's combs on a dark blue ground; bottom band contains an inscription in Armenian: *Khanum 1887.*
Published: Davtian, S., *The Armenian Karpet*, Yerevan, 1975, table XXXIX (in Armenian).

Georgian Pardaghi Carpets

BY TATYANA GRIGOLIYA

Though the weaving of carpets was never as intensive in Georgia as in neighbouring Azerbaijan, Armenia or Daghestan, the names of such carpet-making villages in Eastern Georgia as Karayazy, Karachop and Kosalar, which are near Borchaly, are so well known that they have been incorporated into the universally accepted nomenclature of Caucasian carpets. Georgian pile carpets do not comprise a group of their own but are a sub-group of Azerbaijanian Gianja-Kazakhs, as they have a similar texture.

Old-time Tiflis, today Tbilisi, the capital of the Georgian Soviet Republic, was in the nineteenth century a major trading centre of the Transcaucasus. Exported via Tiflis westward were not only the carpets of Azerbaijan, Armenia and Daghestan but also carpets and rugs manufactured in Central Asia and Northern Persia. As a result, Tiflis carpet-merchants accumulated in their warehouses pieces of various provenance. Owing to their immediate links with the places of manufacture, local carpet-merchants evolved their own nomenclature for Caucasian carpets which in the main is used to this day.

In the nineteenth century in Georgia, unlike in Azerbaijan, Armenia and Daghestan, the manufacture of carpets was not an artisan craft practised for commercial purposes. Pile carpets were made for the market only in Eastern Georgia, in localities inhabited by Armenians and Azerbaijanians as well as by Georgians. The best-known centre of pile weavings is Borchaly.

In areas with a predominantly Georgian population pile carpets were not in common use. Homes were furnished with domestic-made wooden furniture and there was no need to carpet the earthen floors. On the other hand, the making of flat-woven carpets was practised universally. Known in Georgia as *pardaghis*, they were used as wall hangings or to cover benches, couches and sofas. The so-called "horizontal" *pardaghis*, which were embellished with a transverse design and hung above a bench set against the wall, were most common in the Georgian highlands.

The tributaries of the Kura and the Rioni, Georgia's two main rivers, divide Georgia into a great number of districts. Each district had its own type of ornamental design and its own characteristic colour scheme for the *pardaghi*, while Kizyki, a region in Eastern Kakhetia, had its own special technique as well. In the Kizyki *pardaghi* the differently coloured weft threads interlace, thus there is no slit along the warp where the two differently coloured weft threads meet.

Particularly exciting are the *pardaghis* made in the Kakhetian village of Kvemo Alvani along the upper reaches of the Alazani River. Local farmers have preserved at

home many *pardaghis* including some made in the early nineteenth century, and others made perhaps only fifteen or twenty years ago. By the remarkable colouring of these flat-woven carpets alone one can easily attribute them. Alvani peasant women never wove their *pardaghis* for sale, and to this day they are still in the original families' possession. What is still more interesting is that each composition is characteristic of a certain family. Thus, in plate 124 we have *pardaghi* made by the Karkhilauri family and in plate 111 *pardaghi* made by the Idoidze family. In cases when something was made for sale, the family ornamental motif has been lost and all we know is the place from which a given weaving comes.

Though differing in type the *pardaghi* shared a common black-and-white design and a strict colour scheme. Based on the type of design, *pardaghis* may be divided into several groups, as the technique of their making usually called for a horizontal system of rows, and the favourite motif was a geometrically medallion with crosses inscribed in it. These few elements were blended in different ways and alternated in different scales in such a manner that each time the surface design was composed differently.

The loveliness of the flat-woven *pardaghi* carpet lies, however, not so much in vigorous and bold design as in the colour scheme, even though the palette is of a limited nature. All that the village weaver had available was a black thread with a bluish tinge and a white woollen thread. The mid-red, cherry-red, pinks, yellows and browns that are so extensively employed in Armenia and Azerbaijan are introduced only as a supplementary bright spot in the austere, even stark, colour scheme of Georgian carpets.

Because earlier Georgian flat-woven carpets were not made for sale, internationally they are unknown. In this book the reader will find for the first time specimens of such carpets made in different parts of Georgia.

107. PARDAGHI FLAT-WOVEN CARPET. 150×155 cm

From the village of Kvemo Alvani, Akhmet district, Georgia. Early 20th century

In the possession of the Uturgaidze family

Warp and weft: wool.
Dyes: natural.
Finish: selvedges and upper end—no additional working; lower end—warps end in fringe.
Ornament and composition: stitched together from two symmetrical parts; central field carries transverse rows of lozenge-shaped figures with crosses inside each; framed by a border with geometrical pattern; black-and-white colouring is characteristic of all carpets made in this district.
Not published before.

108. PARDAGHI FLAT-WOVEN CARPET. 290×83 cm

By Ye. Karkhilauri

From the village of Vestomta, Akhmet district, Georgia. Second half of 19th century

Museum of Georgian Architecture and Daily Life, Tbilisi. No. 409

Warp and weft: wool.
Dyes: natural.
Finish: selvedges—no additional working; ends—cut; fabric sewn on.
Ornament and composition: central field contains two rows of lozenge-shaped figures separated by a band with pattern identical to that of the border.
Not published before.

109. PARDAGHI FLAT-WOVEN CARPET. 128×166 cm

From the village of Arboshiki, Tsiteli-tskaro district, Georgia. 1920s or 1930s

Museum of the Folk and Applied Arts of the Georgian SSR, Tbilisi. No. 3973

Warp: cotton; *weft:* wool.
Dyes: natural and synthetic.
Finish: selvedges and lower end—no additional working; upper end—strengthened with fabric.
Ornament and composition: central field contains transverse rows of small *buta*, or *boteh*, figures (called *mani* in Georgian) that are characteristically picked out in black; central field framed by a border with floral pattern.
Reproduced is the lower cut-off half.
Not published before.

110. MAIN CARPET. 195×130 cm

From the village of Beshtashen, Tsalkini district, Georgia. About 1930

The Church of the Nativity of the Virgin, Tbilisi

Warp, weft and pile: wool.
Knot: symmetrical; *density:* 1,088 knots per dm² (32×34); *pile height:* 6–7 mm.
Dyes: natural and synthetic.
Finish: selvedges—wool wrapped round two pairs of warps; ends—warps end in fringe.
Ornament and composition: central field contains a large medallion with stylized floral design; this ornament is typical of Beshtashen carpets; central field framed by three borders.
Not published before.

111. PARDAGHI FLAT-WOVEN CARPET. 159×124 cm

From the village of Kvemo Alvani, Akhmet district, Georgia. Early 20th century

In the possession of G. Kandareli, Tbilisi

Warp and weft: wool.
Dyes: natural.
Finish: selvedges—no additional working; ends—warps end in fringe.
Ornament and composition: central field contains graphic design typical of the Idoidze family; topped by illegible inscription in Georgian; central field framed by a border carrying geometrical pattern; torn in several places.
Not published before.

112. PARDAGHI FLAT-WOVEN CARPET. 260×84 cm

From the village of Kvemo Alvani, Akhmet district, Georgia. Early 20th century

In the possession of M. Bakuridze

Warp and weft: wool.
Dyes: natural.
Finish: selvedges—no additional working; ends—warps end in fringe.
Ornament and composition: central field contains three rows of geometrical designs; framed by a white border with geometrical pattern.
Not published before.

113. "HORIZONTAL" PARDAGHI FLAT-WOVEN CARPET (*shadda* technique). 89×284 cm

From the Dusheti district, Khevsuretia, Georgia. Late 19th or early 20th century

Art Museum of Georgia, Tbilisi. No. 892

Warp and weft: wool.
Dyes: natural.
Finish: selvedges—warps end in fringe; ends—no additional working.
Ornament and composition: central field carries a horizontal row of crosses typical of Khevsur carpets; along edge are floral patterns also disposed horizontally; central field framed by a border with geometrical design.
Not published before.

114. "SAMKVAVILA" PARDAGHI FLAT-WOVEN CARPET. 330×160 cm

From the village of Mirzaani, Tsiteli-tskaro district, Georgia. 1930s

The Pirosmanashvili Memorial Museum, Mirzaani. No. 637

Warp: cotton; *weft:* wool.
Dyes: synthetic.
Finish: selvedges—no additional working; ends—warps end in fringe.
Ornament and composition: central field contains three large rhomboidal medallions (*samkvavila* means "three medallions" in Georgian); framed by a border with floral design typical of the district of provenance.
Not published before.

115. PARDAGHI FLAT-WOVEN CARPET. 239×147 cm

From the village of Vaziani, Gurjaani district, Georgia. Early 20th century

In the possession of A. Madzgarashvili

Warp and weft: wool.
Dyes: natural and synthetic.
Finish: selvedges—no additional working; ends—warps end in fringe.
Ornament and composition: central field carries offset rows of identical ornamental motifs of alternating colours; central field framed by two borders with geometrical design; torn in several places.
Not published before.

116. "HORIZONTAL" PARDAGHI FLAT-WOVEN CARPET. Detail.
169×484 cm

From the village of Tsinarehi, Kasp district, Georgia. Early 20th century

Museum of Georgian Architecture and Daily Life, Tbilisi. No. 2289

Warp and weft: wool.
Dyes: natural and synthetic.
Finish: selvedges—warps end in fringe; ends—no additional working.

Ornament and composition: framed central field ornamented with floral design and small geometrical elements.
Not published before.

117. PARDAGHI FLAT-WOVEN CARPET. 198×98 cm

From the village of Kvemo Alvani, Akhmet district, Georgia. 1878–93

Museum of Georgian Architecture and Daily Life, Tbilisi. No. 413

Warp and weft: wool.
Dyes: natural.
Finish: selvedges and ends—no additional working.
Ornament and composition: central field carries lozenge-shaped figures enclosed in zigzag outlines; framed by three borders.

Reproduced is the middle piece of a 6 m long carpet cut into three parts.
Not published before.

118. PARDAGHI FLAT-WOVEN CARPET. 214×99 cm

From the village of Kvemo Alvani, Akhmet district, Georgia. Late 19th century

Museum of Georgian Architecture and Daily Life, Tbilisi. No. 414

Warp and weft: wool.
Dyes: natural.
Finish: selvedges—no additional working; upper end—cut, sewn with fabric; lower end warps end in fringe.
Ornament and composition: black central field carries stylized crosses and toothed lozenges, traditional for the district of provenance; central field framed by a border embellished with black-and-white geometrical motif; frayed in places.

Reproduced is the bottom half of a 4.5 m long carpet.
Not published before.

119. PARDAGHI FLAT-WOVEN CARPET. 276×141 cm

By P. Madzgarashvili

From the village of Mirzaani, Tsiteli-tskaro district, Georgia. 1929

In the possession of A. Madzgarashvili

Warp and weft: wool.
Dyes: natural and synthetic.
Finish: selvedges—no additional working; ends—warps end in fringe.
Ornament and composition: central field carries rows of *buta* figures shaped in a manner characteristic of the district of

provenance; framed by a border with floral design that is typical for the *pardaghis* of this district; torn in several places.
Not published before.

120. PARDAGHI FLAT-WOVEN CARPET. 211×82 cm

From the village of Kvemo Alvani, Akhmet district, Georgia. 1920

In the possession of A. Cholikaidze, Kvemo Alvani

Warp and weft: wool.

Dyes: natural.
Finish: selvedges—no additional working; upper end—cut, sewn with fabric; lower end—warps end in fringe.
Ornament and composition: central field carries white graphic design with coloured lozenges in traditional soft tints characteristic of carpets made in this district; central field framed by a border with geometrical design; torn in several places.
Reproduced is the lower cut-off half.
Not published before.

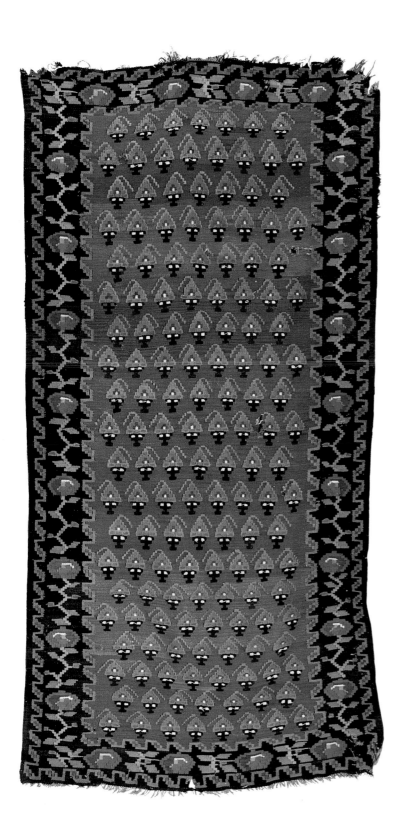

21. MAIN CARPET. 220×156 cm

From the village of Karayazy, Borchaly District, Georgia. About 1880

Art Museum of Georgia, Tbilisi. No. 2613

Warp, weft and pile: wool.
Knot: asymmetrical; *density:* 1,152 knots per m² (32×36); *pile height:* 4 mm.
Dyes: natural.
Finish: selvedges—wool wrapped round two pairs of warps; ends—1.5 cm plain weave, fringe.
Ornament and composition: central field carries four large stylized birds around a cruciform medallion; at top and bottom are three rows of geometrical designs; framed by four borders embellished with black-and-white ornamental design that is typical of the area of provenance; this type of carpet is woven in villages inhabited by Georgians, Armenians and Azerbaijanians.
Not published before.

22. PARDAGHI FLAT-WOVEN CARPET. 337×173 cm

From the village of Khevsurtsopeli, Tianeti District, Georgia. 1935

Museum of the Folk and Applied Arts of the Georgian SSR, Tbilisi. No. 2025

Warp: cotton; *weft:* wool.
Dyes: natural and synthetic.
Finish: selvedges—no additional working; ends—warps end in fringe.
Ornament and composition: imitation of the Achma-Yumma Karabakh; along top is an inscription in Georgian: *1935, 9 July, woven by Maro Katsiashvili*; central field framed by a border ornamented with the reworked motif of an embroidery print pattern.
Not published before.

123. PARDAGHI FLAT-WOVEN CARPET. 240×116 cm

From the village of Tianeti, Tetritskaroi district, Georgia. 1979

"Solani" Folk Arts and Crafts Workshop, Georgia, Tbilisi

Warp and weft: cotton.
Dyes: natural.
Colours: six—dark red, dark green, black, light green, light red, white.
Finish: selvedges—no additional working; ends—warps end in fringe.
Ornament and composition: central field contains a large medallion with floral and geometrical designs; framed by a border ornamented with floral design.
Not published before.

124. PARDAGHI FLAT-WOVEN CARPET. 163×100 cm

By E. Jijuridze

From the village of Kvemo Alvani, Akhmet district, Georgia. 1978

In the possession of the E. Jijuridze family, Tbilisi

Warp and weft: cotton.
Dyes: natural and synthetic.
Colours: six—white, black, dark blue, dark red, light green, violet.
Finish: selvedges and upper end—no additional working; lower end—warps end in fringe.
Ornament and composition: central field contains two rows of X-shaped figures flanking a row of lozenge-shaped figures (this pattern is traditional for the Karkhilauri family); central field framed by a border ornamented with geometrical motif.
Not published before.

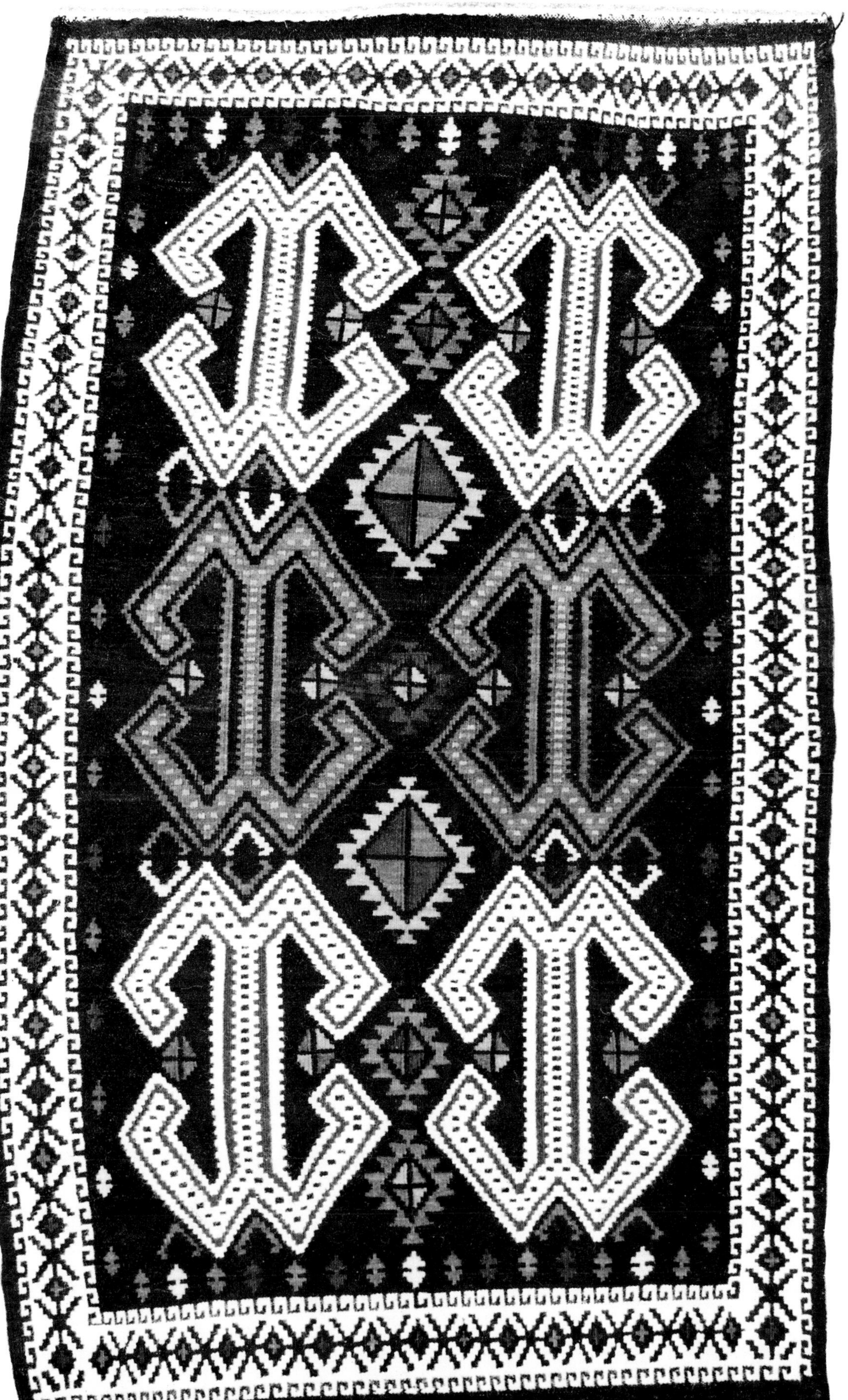

BIBLIOGRAPHY

Abdullayeva, N. A., "Historical Outline of the Development of the Carpet-making Art in Soviet Azerbaijan (1920–29)," in: *Proceedings of the Academy of Sciences of the Azerbaijan SSR*, No. 8, 1961 (in Azerbaijani)

Achdjian, A., Achdjian, B., *Tapis d'Orient anciens*, Paris, 1979

Adamov, A. K., *Soviet Carpets and Their Export*, Moscow, Leningrad, 1934 [Адамов, А. К., *Советские ковры и их экспорт*, Москва, Ленинград, 1934]

Aliyeva, A. S., "The Development of Azerbaijan's Carpet-making Art in the 19th and 20th Centuries," in: *Proceedings of the Academy of Sciences of the Azerbaijan SSR*, No. 1, 1968 (in Azerbaijani)

Aliyeva, K. M., "On Study of Flat-woven Azerbaijanian Carpets," in: *Proceedings of the Academy of Sciences of the Azerbaijan SSR*, No. 3, 1972 (in Azerbaijani)

Ausstellung Kaukasische Teppiche, Frankfurt, 1962

Bausback, P., *Antike orientalische Knüpfkunst*, 1976

Bode, W., *Anciens tapis d'Orient*, Paris, 1902

Bode, W., Kühnel, E., *Antique Rugs from the Near East*, London, 1970

Caladtoni, R., *Tapis d'Orient (histoire, esthétique, symbolisme)*, Paris, 1967

"Carpet-making in the Kuba District of the Baku Province," *Cottage Industries in the Caucasus*, Issue 1, Tiflis, 1902

["Ковровый промысел в Кубинском уезде Бакинской губернии, *Кустарная промышленность на Кавказе*, вып. 1, Тифлис, 1902]

Davtian, S., *The Armenian Karpet*, Yerevan, 1975 (in Armenian)

Davtian, S., *Outline History of Medieval Armenian Applied Arts*, Yerevan, 1981 (in Armenian)

Dimand, M. S. and Mailey, J., *Oriental Rugs in the Metropolitan Museum of Art*, New York, 1973

Edwards, C. A., *The Persian Carpet*, London, 1975

Erdmann, K., *Seven Hundred Years of Oriental Carpets*, London, 1972

Erdmann, K., *Oriental Carpets*, New York, 1962

Fahrenkamp, G., *Antiquitäten-Teppiche, Knüpfteppiche aus Persien, Kleinasien, dem Kaukasus, Zentralasien und Ostasien*, Munich, 1974

Fokker, N., *Persian and Other Oriental Carpets for Today*, London, 1973

Gayayan, A., "13th- 15th-century Armenian Carpets in Cappadoce," in: *Second Symposium on Armenian Art. A Collection of Reports*, Yerevan, 1981, vol. 3, pp. 246–257, ill. 95–101 [Гаяян А., "Армянские ковры XIII–XV веков в Каппадокии, в кн.: *II Международный симпозиум по армянскому искусству. Сборник докладов*, Ереван, 1981, т. 3, с. 246–257, ил. 95–101]

Gogel, V. F., *Carpets*, Moscow, 1950 [Гогель В. Ф., *Ковры*, М., 1950]

Gombos, K., *Les Tapis anciens arméniens*, Budapest, 1975

Grote-Hasenbald, W., *Teppiche aus dem Orient*, Leipzig, 1936

Hofrichter, Z., *Armenische Teppiche*, Wien, 1937

Hubel, P. W., *The Book of Carpets*, New York and Washington, 1970

Isayev, M. D., *Carpet Manufacture in Transcaucasia*, Tiflis, 1932 [Исаев М. Д. *Ковровое производство Закавказья*, Тифлис, 1932]

Kerimov, L. G., "Notes of a Carpet Designer," *Decorative Art in the USSR*, 1959, No. 9 [Керимов Л. Г., "Заметки художника-орнаменталиста", *Декоративное искусство СССР*, 1959, № 9]

Kerimov, L. G., *The Azerbaijanian Carpet*, vol. 1, Baku, Leningrad, 1961 [Керимов Л. Г., *Азербайджанский ковер*, т. 1, Баку, Ленинград, 1961]

Kilchevskaya, E. V., Ivanov, A. S., *The Handicrafts of Daghestan*, Moscow, 195 [Кильчевская Э. В., Иванов А. С., *Художественные промыслы Дагестана*, Москва, 1959]

Landreau, A. N., Pickering, W. R., *From th Bosporus to Samarkand: Flat-woven Rugs*, Washington, D.C., 1969

Lefevre, J., *Caucasian Carpets*, London, 197

Lettermair, J. G., *Das Große Orientteppichbuch*, Munich, 1962

"Lyatif Kerimov's Classification of the Rugs Azerbaijan," *Hali*, vol. 3, No. 1, 1980

Markgraf, O. V., *An Outline of the Cottage Industries in the Northern Caucasus*, Moscow, 1882 [Маркграф О. В., *Очерк кустарных промыслов Северного Кавказа*, Москва, 1882]

Martin, F. R., *A History of Oriental Carpets before 1800*, Vienna, 1908

Martin, F. R., "The Classification of Oriental Rugs," *The Burlington Magazine*, London, 1905/6, VIII

Maruashvili, L., *Tusheti*, Tbilisi, 1977 (in Georgian)

McMullan, J. V., *Islamic Carpets*, New York, 1965

McMullan, J. V., Reichert, D. O., *The George Walter Vincent and Belle Townsley Smith Collection of Islamic Rugs*, Springfield, 1970

Miller, A. A., *Carpet Products of the East. An Exhibition of the Ethnography Department of the Russian Museum*, Leningrad, 1924 [Миллер А. А., *Ковровые изделия Востока. Выставка этнографического отдела Русского музея*, Ленинград, 1924]

Mohameds, Sh., *Kleine Geschichte über die Entstehung der Perserteppiche*, 1974

Mujiri, J. M., *Carpet-weaving in Azerbaijan*, Baku, 1977 [Муджири Дж. М., *Ковроткачество Азербайджана*, Баку, 1977]

Neugebauer, R., Orendi, J., *Handbuch der orientalischen Teppichkunde*, Leipzig, 1923

Peter, W., Meister, E., *Kaukasische Teppiche*, Brunswick, 1961

Piralov, A. S., *A Sketch of Caucasian Cottage Industries*, St. Petersburg, 1913 [Пиралов А. С., *Краткий очерк кустарных промыслов Кавказа*, Спб., 1913]

Riegel, A., *Ein orientalischer Teppich vom Jahre 1202 n. Chr. und die ältesten orientalischen Teppiche*, Berlin, 1895

Riegel, A., *Altorientalische Teppiche*, Leipzig, 1891

Ropers, H., *Morgenländische Teppiche*, Brunswick, 1965

Ruedin, E. J., *The Connoisseur's Guide to Oriental Carpets*, Tokyo, 1971

Sakissian, A., "Les tapis arméniens du XVᵉ au XIXᵉ siècle", *La Revue de l'art ancien et moderne*, 1933, vol. LXIV, juin, p. 346

Sakissian, A., "Les tapis à dragon et leur origine arménienne", *Syria*, 1928, p. 254

Schürmann, U., *Teppiche aus dem Kaukasus*, 1964

Stebling, E., *The Holy Carpet of the Mosque at Andebie*, London, 1892

Temurjan, V., *Carpet-making in Armenia*, Yerevan, 1955 (in Armenian)

Veimarn, B., "Carpets of the Soviet East," *Arts*, 1947, No. 2 [Веймарн Б., "Ковры Советского Востока, *Искусство*, 1947, № 2]

Victoria and Albert Museum. Fifty Masterpieces of Textiles, London, 1951

"Weaving, Dyeing, Embroidery," in: *Materials on the History of Folk Cottage Industries and Petty Handicrafts in Georgia*

(Collection of articles edited by Academician I. A. Dzhavakhishvili), Tbilisi, 1982, vol. 2, part 2 (in Georgian)

Zedgenidze, Ya., "The Making of Carpets and Palases in Shusha," in: *Collection of Materials for Describing Caucasian Localities and Tribes*, Issue 11, Tiflis, 1891 [Зедгенидзе Я., "Производство ковров и паласов в г. Шуше", в кн.: *Сборник материалов для описания местностей и племен Кавказа*, вып. 11, Тифлис, 1891]

Zummer, V. M., "Modern Kuba Carpets," in: *The Transactions of the Society for the Survey and Study of Azerbaijan*, Baku, 1926 [Зуммер В. М., "Современные кубинские ковры", в кн.: *Известия общества обследования и изучения Азербайджана*, Баку, 1926]

КОВРЫ КАВКАЗА

Альбом (на английском языке)

ИЗДАТЕЛЬСТВО „АВРОРА". ЛЕНИНГРАД. 1984
Изд. № 672. (7-20)
PRINTED AND BOUND IN AUSTRIA BY GLOBUS, VIENNA